**Project Management Institute**

# MIDDLE MANAGERS IN PROGRAM AND PROJECT PORTFOLIO MANAGEMENT

*Practices, Roles and Responsibilities*

**Project Management Institute**

# MIDDLE MANAGERS IN PROGRAM AND PROJECT PORTFOLIO MANAGEMENT
## *Practices, Roles and Responsibilities*

Tomas Blomquist, PhD
Ralf Müller, DBA

ISBN: 1-930699-57-3

Published by:     Project Management Institute, Inc.
                  Four Campus Boulevard
                  Newtown Square, Pennsylvania 19073-3299 USA.
                  Phone: +610-356-4600
                  Fax: +610-356-4647
                  E-mail: pmihq@pmi.org
                  Internet: www.pmi.org

10  9  8  7  6  5  4  3  2  1

# Table of Contents

# Acknowledgements

This study was initiated by the Project Management Institute (PMI) as one of its activities to foster the advancement of project, program, and portfolio management. The authors are deeply indebted to PMI for their support and guidance throughout the study.

We should give particular mention to Dr. Harry Stefanou from the PMI Project Management Research Program and to Prof. Dragan Milosević for their guidance, as well as Wanda Curlee and Shelley Gaddie from the Project Management Research Member Advisory Group (RMAG) for their valuable contributions. We are especially grateful to our Research Coordinator, Eva Goldman, for her continuous support during the entire life cycle of the study.

Further support was provided by the Research Institute of Umeå School of Business and Economics, Umeå University, Umeå, Sweden. Through additional funding and provision of the school's facilities and technology, we were able to finish the study in the timeframe set in the beginning and reach our quality objectives. Special thanks are extended to Prof. Anders Söderholm, Prof. Maria Bengtsson, Prof. Kurt Brännäs and Associate Prof. Nils Wåhlin from Umeå University for their support of the study.

During our presentation of the study results to the research community, we received a number of helpful recommendations and hints. We also thank attendees of the PMI Research Conference 2004 in London, UK, for their helpful comments on the subject.

An empirical study like this would not have been possible without the voluntary help of practitioners, who devote their time and knowledge to the advancement of the profession. We thank, in particular, the interviewees and questionnaire respondents for taking the time and effort to share their knowledge with us, as well as those who provided further comments and descriptions of their program and portfolio management practices.

Many more than we can mention here have helped us behind the scenes, including our families and friends. We could not have done this study without their help.

# Executive Summary

What are middle managers' roles and responsibilities in program and project portfolio management? What are the best practices of successful companies today? These questions are of increasing interest for organizations operating with limited resources and ambitious performance objectives. More and more organizations use projects as the building blocks for their business in order to deliver unique products or services to their clients' specific requirements. At the same time, organizations are required to optimize the use of their resources to achieve their own business objectives. These project-based organizations have to balance two competing objectives: the delivery of high quality project and program objectives to internal and external clients, and the most economic assignment of their resources across all projects in the organization.

The majority of past studies looked into program and portfolio management to identify which project selection technique is most successful, how Return-on-Investment (ROI) decisions are made, or which planning techniques are appropriate. The present study looks at the middle managers' roles and responsibilities in program and portfolio management. Through that, the study takes an organizational-wide perspective towards the subject and identifies the best practices of successful companies. To that end, the study is complementary to existing literature written solely from a program or portfolio management perspective, and produces the activities, processes, and tools used for successful program and portfolio management in an organization.

Results from the study suggest that successful companies engage in both program and portfolio management simultaneously, in order to balance the variety of requirements from their internal and external clients. Success of these organizations is significantly higher than for organizations with neither program nor portfolio management, or those with only one of these two governance structures. Middle managers in successful organizations are significantly more involved in steering group work, resource procurement, identification of bad projects, handling of issues related to programs and portfolios, as well as review and audit of troubled projects.

The framework of program and portfolio management roles of middle managers, developed through this study, shows how effectiveness, efficiency, and coordination are achieved through a set of activities prior to and during project execution. To manage their portfolio of projects, middle managers identify business opportunities, look for synergies between projects, and plan for and select required resources before projects are executed. During the same time, business planning, project selection, resource planning and procurement, and program plan reviews take place in order to manage the programs of the organization. During project execution, middle managers are engaged in identification of bad projects, participation in steering groups, coordination, and issue handling.

Results show further that organizations apply these roles to balance the complexity and dynamics of their environment. Low performing organizations show a lack of adaptability to situational changes, which leads to an imbalance in their ability to handle product, time, and complexity requirements from their clients.

This report is written for a wide variety of readers, such as senior executives and middle managers in larger organizations, program and portfolio managers, PMO members, consultants, and researchers. These groups have different perspectives towards the subject and expect different information from this report. To meet their specific areas of interest, we provide a short summary of each chapter. This allows readers to quickly identify those parts of the report that meet their information needs and expectations. However, to comprehend the study in its entirety, it is suggested that one reads the whole report.

The following summarizes the chapters in this report.

## Introduction and Background

This chapter describes the motivation and context of the study. By taking an organization-wide perspective, the chapter describes program and portfolio management as a governance structure for project-based organizations. Individual projects within this structure are seen as transactions, which efficiently and effectively convert "input" to "output." To accommodate the different governance structures required for management of a variety of simultaneous projects in an organization, the study takes on a Transaction Cost Economics (TCE) perspective. Based on this theoretical foundation, the chapter outlines the research questions, which set out to:

- Identify the impact of an organization's complexity on the application of program and portfolio management
- Identify the practices, roles, and responsibilities of middle managers in program and portfolio management of successful organizations.

Following that, the study's plan, schedule, milestone deliverables, and team are described.

## Literature Review

This chapter summarizes the underlying literature of this study. It starts by outlining definitions of portfolios and their management, then the literature is grouped by popular project selection techniques, different planning and management techniques and their associated problems, and competencies needed for portfolio management. Similarly, the program management literature is reviewed by outlining the objectives of programs and program management, and then categorizing literature into groups addressing aspects of program organization, program life cycles, and competencies needed for managing programs of projects.

Neither programs nor portfolios exist in a vacuum. Therefore, the literature on project types, as well as organizational complexity, is briefly reviewed to identify factors that may impact the application of program and portfolio management structures in an organization.

The chapter ends by outlining the four hypotheses of the study, which address:

- The relationship of an organization's complexity with the use of program and portfolio management
- The correlation of different project types with different program and portfolio management roles and responsibilities
- The difference in governance structures for program and portfolio management in low and high performing organizations
- The difference of middle managers' roles and responsibilities in program and portfolio management between low and high performing organizations.

## Methodology and Analysis

This chapter outlines the multi-method approach underlying the study. It starts by describing how a first qualitative study with nine interviews was used to build a grounded theory, which was then confirmed through a global qualitative study with 242 responses, and triangulated with other study results. The underlying research paradigm, development of the different data gathering tools, and samples of the studies are described, together with the techniques used to analyze the collected data.

Analyses of the two studies are described in detail. They begin by showing the development of a framework for roles and responsibilities through the first study. This framework identifies the different ways that middle managers engage in program and portfolio management prior to and during project execution to coordinate tasks, as well as manage effectiveness and efficiency of project work. Analysis of the data from the second study confirms this framework. It shows the roles and responsibilities of middle managers and the organizational program and portfolio management structures of successful organizations, and how these are impacted by an organization's complexity. Modeling the relationship between organizational complexity, project types, and program and portfolio management roles identifies the situational adaptability of an organization as a key factor in structuring an organization for high performance. Results triangulation is done by mapping the present study's results against those of other studies, in order to identify overlaps and differences.

This chapter is mainly written for readers interested in the details of the underlying research process and analysis techniques. The results of the various analyses are described in the next chapter.

## Managerial Implications: What Middle Managers in Successful Organizations Do

This chapter summarizes the results of the two studies and describes:
- The practices, roles, and responsibilities in the framework developed in the prior chapter
- The differences between high and low performing programs and portfolios
- The impact of organizational complexity on the structures to successfully organize for program and portfolio management.

Managerial implications and recommendations for organizations and middle managers are discussed. Recommendations for further reading are provided.

## Theoretical Implications and Conclusions

This chapter sets the study results in context of the research questions outlined in the introductory chapter. A contingency model is developed, which is derived from the research model described in the methodology chapter. It shows the impact of project type and organizational complexity variables on variables for middle managers practices, roles, and responsibilities in program and portfolio management. Theoretical implications are elaborated from this, and the study's contributions to existing theories are provided. Strength and weaknesses of the study are provided, as well as suggestions for future research. The report finishes by setting the results of the study in a wider context and a vision for the future.

The Appendices provide the interview questions, the global Web-based questionnaire, and some of the statistical summary tables of the data analysis.

# CHAPTER 1

# Introduction and Background

> Throughout the latter half of the 20th century, there has been a shift in the management paradigm, from the functional, bureaucratic approach, almost universally adopted in the first half of the century, to project and process-based approaches. This shift has been in response to the changing nature of the work from mass production, with essentially stable customer requirements and slowly changing technology, to the current situation where every product supplied may be against a bespoke [custom-made] design, and technology changes continuously and rapidly (Turner & Keegan, 1999, p. 296).

More and more organizations organize their work by projects in order to achieve their business objectives most economically. This leads to a steady increase in the number of simultaneous projects in organizations. Through that, a need arises to manage these simultaneous projects from an organizational perspective. Recent years have shown that two distinct management approaches are primarily used for that purpose; these are program and project portfolio management. However, neither management approach is uniform, and they need to be adapted to each organization's particular situation, based on its environment and business type. Along with differences in program and portfolio management approaches, the practices, roles, and responsibilities of middle managers in these organizations vary.

Middle managers have been the target in downsizing activities of organizations for many decades. While they diminish in number, they continue to hold a pivotal position at the crossroads of strategic thinking and operational implementation in organizations. Being perceived as problems solvers, they have to balance a multitude of requirements stemming from their supervisors (e.g., CEOs or management boards), their peers in neighboring organizations (e.g., department managers and vice presidents), and their subordinates (e.g., the first line managers of teams, groups, or projects). Middle managers are often seen as the "real" managers, due to their capability of converting strategy in day-to-day operations, and their role as advocates of whatever group they are working with. They do this by building coalitions between groups and networks of resources. Throughout recent years, middle managers have been asked to cope with the increasing use of projects as a way to do business in organizations. The present study shows the results from an empirical investigation in middle managers' approaches to cope with this increasing "projectification" of organizations. It shows the practices, roles, and responsibilities of middle managers in program and portfolio management in project-based organizations.

Through its vision and interaction with members, as well as their different management groups, the PMI Project Management Research Program identified the need for a better understanding of the current practices, roles, and responsibilities of middle managers in program and portfolio management. The authors of this report were commissioned to execute a study, and this report provides the results. The report is intended to provide a complementary view to the existing literature on program and portfolio management, by focusing on middle managers in project-based organizations. This chapter describes the study context, underlying theoretical foundation, and research questions.

## Program and Portfolio Management as a Subset of Corporate Governance

Program and portfolio management are approaches that structure and execute groups of projects in organizations. As such, they are part of an organization's overall governance structure. Corporate governance is defined by the Organisation for Economic Co-operation and Development (OECD) as:

> . . . one key element in improving economic efficiency and growth as well as enhancing investor confidence. Corporate governance involves a set of relationships between a company's management, its board, its shareholders and other stakeholders. Corporate governance also provides the structure through which the objectives of the company are set, and the means of attaining those objectives and monitoring performance are determined. (2004, p. 11)

Being solely related to project activities, program and portfolio management become a subset of corporate governance known as the *governance of project management*, which, according to the Association for Project Management (APM):

> ... concerns those areas of corporate governance that are specifically related to project activities. Effective governance of project management ensures that an organization's project portfolio is aligned to the organization's objectives, is delivered efficiently and is sustainable. Governance of project management also supports the means by which the board, and other major project stakeholders, are provided with timely, relevant and reliable information. (2004, p. 4)

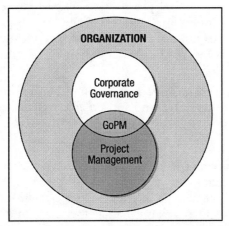

Figure 1     Governance of Project Management in Context

Figure 1, adopted from APM (2004), shows the relationship of organization, corporate governance, governance of project management, and project management. Here, governance of project management addresses the areas of overlap between corporate governance and project management. That includes program and portfolio management.

The main components of this governance structure for project management are (APM, 2004):

- *Portfolio direction effectiveness and efficiency.* This ensures that all projects are identified within one portfolio, or one of the portfolios. A portfolio should be evaluated and directed with the organization's aims and constraints in mind.
- *Project sponsorship effectiveness and efficiency.* This ensures the effective link between senior executives and project management in the organization. Sponsors have decision-making,

directing and representational accountabilities. Project managers report to sponsors, who own the project's business case.

- *Project management effectiveness and efficiency.* This ensures that the teams responsible for projects are capable of achieving the project objectives. That includes skills and knowledge of the project team, project managers, and leaders, but also the resources available to them, their tools and processes, together with the ability to deploy them.
- *Disclosure and reporting.* This ensures the exchange of timely, relevant, and reliable information to support decision-making processes in an organization.

Program and portfolio management address the question of governance from two parallel perspectives. The first perspective takes into account the interconnectedness of the various project objectives in order to maximize accomplishment of combined project outcomes. This has led to the development of programs, which PMI defines as:

> a group of related projects, managed in a coordinated way to obtain benefits and control not available from managing them individually (Project Management Institute [PMI] 2004, p. 368).

The second perspective is concerned with the interrelationships among the management requirements of these projects, in order to achieve the organization's overall business results. This has led to the development of portfolio management techniques, which PMI (2004, p. 367) defines as:

> The centralized management of one or more portfolios, which includes identifying, prioritizing, authorizing, managing, and controlling projects, programs, and other related work, to achieve specific strategic business objectives.

A portfolio is defined as:

> A collection of projects or programs and other work that are grouped together to facilitate effective management of that work to meet strategic business objectives. The projects or programs of the portfolio may not necessarily be interdependent or directly related (PMI 2004, p. 367).

Past research on portfolio management has focused mostly on the management of R&D portfolios. However, as stated in the beginning, other industries increasingly use project-based organizational structures as well, in order to accomplish corporate objectives. This led to the application of portfolio management techniques in new areas such as customer-delivery projects, or for shorter and less capital-intensive projects. This trend contributes to a rapid increase in the number of projects in an organization. Portfolios of these projects are managed differently. Here, factors such as a customer's program size and supplier priorities are taken into account. Approaches to portfolio management, therefore, are contingent on, for example, size and complexity of projects and programs.

Even though program and portfolio management are frequently described in the literature, there is no clear evidence of the way both governance structures are implemented in different organizations, and what the corresponding practices, roles, and responsibilities of the organizations' managers are.

## Governance and Transaction Cost Economics

Program and portfolio management are governance structures adopted to minimize the overall costs in converting "input" to "output" through projects. When viewing projects as transactions, these costs are known as transaction costs, which are the sum of all costs for governing projects. Williamson (1985, p. 18) explains that:

> ... transaction costs are economized by assigning transactions (which differ in their attributes) to governance structures (the adaptive capacities and associated costs which differ) in a discriminating way.

From a similar perspective, in his Transaction Cost Economics (TCE), Williamson (1985) explains the balance required in organizational governance mechanisms to:
- Provide a product's "fit for purpose" by lowering maladaptation costs (i.e., such as done through program management), and
- Lower the costs for the organization by economizing existing scales and resources (i.e., such as in portfolio management).

This identifies program and portfolio management as the linkage between corporate governance and TCE. However, Williamson's TCE claims that different governance structures are required in different types of transactions. The extent that organizations apply program and portfolio management as governance practices is, therefore, seen to differ by project type.

Moreover, the choice of governance structure is described by Williamson (1975) as contingent on the complexity of the environment of an organization. Based on Simon's 1957 *bounded rationality* argument that humans exercise intended, but only limited, rational behavior in decision-making, Williamson (1975, p. 22-23) states that:

> It is bounded rationality in relation to the condition of the environment that occasions the economic problem. [. . .]

When, [however,] transactions are conducted under conditions of uncertainty/complexity, in which event it is very costly, perhaps impossible, to describe the complete decision tree, the bounded rationality constraint is binding and an assessment of alternative organizational modes, in efficiency respects, becomes necessary.

Thus, governance structures are also seen to differ by the degree of uncertainty/complexity of an organization.

## Research Questions

The above leads to the first research question:

*Q1: How do project type and organizational complexity determine the use of project portfolio and program management in organizations?*

Along with differences in projects and the associated application of program and portfolio management in organizations, the roles and responsibilities of the respective managers differ.

That leads to the second research question:

*Q2: What are middle managers' practices, roles, and responsibilities in program and portfolio management in successful organizations?*

The scope and differences of these roles and responsibilities, in relation to organizations' governance structures, are investigated through this study.

## Objectives

The study's objective is to allow middle managers in organizations to improve their practices, roles, and responsibilities in program and portfolio management for the benefit of their organizations, the economy, and, ultimately, society in general. For academics, the objective is to contribute to a refined theory on program and portfolio management structures and their contingency on environmental factors such as organizational complexity and project types.

Another objective is to encourage further research in this field, possibly building on the results of this study, in order to develop an overarching theory of program and portfolio management. That will contribute to the standardization of program and portfolio management practices, the improvement of project management methodologies, and creation of organizational project management maturity models

## Scope and Underlying Assumptions of this Study

The scope of this study is limited to answering the research questions stated in the introductory chapter. The unit of analysis in this study is the middle manager with his/her roles and responsibilities in program and portfolio-related management work. All practices, roles, and responsibilities of these managers outside of program and portfolio management-related work are excluded from the study.

Assumptions underlying this report are:

- Readers are interested in the study results and not in the details of underlying methods and analytical techniques. The report, therefore, mainly provides references to underlying methods, and does not explain them in detail. Readers interested in these details are referred to the references chapter of the report.
- Findings from this study are applicable across industries. No attempt was made to distinguish between different industries. The data collected support this assumption. It is, however, advisable to conduct more industry-specific research in that area in the future
- There is no response bias through the use of electronic media. It is assumed that electronic media such as Internet and e-mail are globally available to middle managers, so that distribution of a questionnaire through the Internet will not cause a response bias among the participants.

## Management Process

The study started with a review of program and portfolio management literature, mainly selected through online databases such as EBSCO, Science Direct, and other academic databases. The review focused on high-quality, peer-reviewed journals, such as *Project Management Journal, International Journal of Project Management, Academy of Management Journal, European Management Journal, Administrative Science Quarterly*, etc.

Following that, a two-step multi-method approach was executed. It started with a qualitative study using a grounded theory approach to develop a first theory on the subject. That was followed by a global qualitative study, which confirmed the findings of the first study, and provided insight into the contextual factors impacting the depth of program and portfolio management use in organizations. The analysis results were triangulated with research results from the University of Technology Helsinki, Finland, and supported the overall findings of the study. The two-step multi-method approach with subsequent triangulation contributed to the credibility of the results.

The details of the research process are outlined in the methodology chapter.

The core team of the study involved two researchers:

Dr. Tomas Blomquist, Principal Investigator
Umeå School of Business and Economics
Umeå University
901 87 Umeå, Sweden
E-mail: tomas.blomquist@fek.umu.se
Phone: +46 90 786 7722

Dr. Ralf Müller
Umeå School of Business and Economics
Umeå University
901 87 Umeå, Sweden
E-mail: ralf.mueller@fek.umu.se
Phone +46 40 689 1312

Throughout the course of the 18-month project, the team kept close contact by either working together at Umeå University or through daily contact in times of joint activities. The project was regularly reported and discussed with the PMI Research Program Manager and RMAG, both through e-mails, phone calls, and face-to-face meetings. Progress was reported through a monthly report to the Research Program Management Team.

## Milestones and Deliverables

The study commenced in October 2003, with the initial planning and setup of interviews. The qualitative study was conducted between November 2003 and March 2004. Following that, the questionnaire for the quantitative study was planned, piloted, distributed, and data collected until December 2004. Analysis of the quantitative data and results triangulation took place in December 2004 and January 2005. Subsequently, the final report was developed.

During the course of the study, the results were continuously communicated to the community of researchers and practitioners, and feedback was sought on the validity of the approach and results. Public presentations and publications include:

- A presentation at the PMI Sweden Chapter's seminar on Program and Portfolio Management, March 2004.
- A conference paper and presentation at the Global Project and Manufacturing Management Symposium, University of Siegen, Germany, May 2004 (Müller & Blomquist, 2004).

- A conference paper and presentation at the PMI Research Conference 2004 in London, July 2004 (Blomquist & Müller, 2004a).
- A presentation at the PMI Sweden Chapter's seminar on Program, Portfolio Management and Maturity, September 2004.
- A chapter in Slevin, Cleland, and Pinto's book *Innovations: Project management research 2004* (Blomquist & Müller, 2004b).
- A journal article submitted to *Project Management Journal* that is currently under review (Blomquist & Müller, 2005a).
- This research report.

Table 1 outlines the major milestones and deliverables.

| Milestone | Completion Date |
| --- | --- |
| Interviews | 13 January 04 |
| Analysis of interviews | 12 March 04 |
| PMI Research Conference paper | 15 March 04 |
| PMI Sweden Chapter workshop | 23 March 04 |
| Project Mgmt. Conference paper, Germany | 06 May 04 |
| PMI Research book chapter | 12 July 04 |
| Survey pilot | 26 September 04 |
| PMI Sweden chapter workshop | 28 September 04 |
| Final survey data collected | 10 December 04 |
| Survey analysis completed | 14 January 05 |
| Journal paper submitted to *Project Management Journal* | 28 January 05 |
| Monograph completed | 31 March 05 |

Table 1    Study Milestones and Deliverables

## Supporting Organizations

This research study was supported by two organizations:
- PMI's Project Management Research Program initiated the study and provided overall guidance, as well as parts of the financial support
- Umeå University, through its Research Institute at the Umeå School of Business and Economics, provided facilities and technology to conduct the study, as well as parts of the financial support.

## Report Structure

The next chapter reviews the literature on program and portfolio management, as well as on organizational complexity.

This is followed by a chapter describing the research methodology and data gathering techniques, and a chapter with analysis of the collected data.

Those chapters are then followed by a discussion of the results in a chapter on managerial implications, and the report concludes with a chapter on theoretical implications, including a final model for program and portfolio management in organizations, as well as recommendations for further research.

# CHAPTER 2

# Literature Review

---

This chapter reviews the literature on program and portfolio management, as well as project type and environmental complexity. A review, however, can only cover a subset of the literature written on a subject (Hart, 1998). The intent with this chapter, therefore, is to identify the major theories, tools, and techniques developed in program and portfolio management. To that end, the review focuses on four sets of literature: program management, portfolio management, project types, and organizational complexity. Within each of these categories, the literature is grouped by dominant subject areas. The review ends with an identification of a gap in the existing literature when it comes to answering the research questions, and identifies a set of hypotheses that guide the remainder of the research study. Parts of this review have been published before in Blomquist & Müller (2004b).

## Project Portfolios and Their Management

Project portfolios provide frameworks for management to compare a variety of different projects in order to decide in which one to invest. Portfolio techniques were originally developed by General Electric/McKinsey and Boston Consulting Group (BCG), and showed a business's competitive position and market prospects in a matrix or grid. Different positions on the grid suggested different marketing strategies, as in Figure 2 (Goold & Luchs, 1996). From such a corporate perspective, the optimum portfolio was often defined as one in which the products in the Cash Cows quadrant generate adequate cash flows to produce sufficient returns for shareholders, as well as cash to further develop the products in the Question Marks and Stars quadrants to replace the Cash Cows in the future. For such portfolios

---

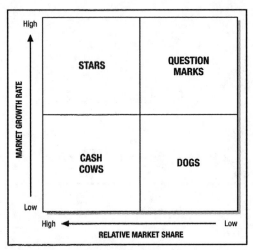

Figure 2　　　BCG Market Growth / Relative Share Matrix

to be manageable, it is necessary that products be linked in a way that allows benefiting from the organization's competencies (Scott, 1997).

Over time, the technique became a standard method for selecting projects for organizations. Research & Development (R&D) organizations especially used the technique to guide the decisions for project selection and resource assignments. To that end, portfolio management helped to *do the right projects*, whereas the complementary project management methods were used to *do projects right* (Cooper, Edgett, & Kleinschmidt., 2000).

With the increasing use of projects as a means to deliver products and services, the use of portfolio management techniques for governance of resource-interrelated projects steadily increased. Here, portfolio management techniques are used to guide organizations' management decisions on prioritization of resource assignments across projects (for example, maximization of economic value, "fire fighting" troubled projects, minimizing risks, and maximizing a project's long-term ROI).

Literature on portfolio management was found to address three major perspectives:

- Portfolio definitions and associated project selection techniques
- Planning and management of project portfolios
- Competencies for portfolio management.

Each of these three categories of literature is discussed in the following section.

### Portfolio Definitions and Selection Techniques

With the increased use of projects as a development and delivery process for products and services, the management methods of *doing a project right* have turned into an organizational issue of *doing the right projects*. Project portfolios, as methods for decision-making across projects (e.g., through selection of projects and resource allocation between projects), becomes increasingly important for organizations in achieving their strategic objectives. This discussion emerged first in the R&D literature (Baker & Freeland, 1975; Schmidt & Freeland, 1992; Chien 2002).

The most popular model for portfolio definition was empirically developed by Cooper et al. (1997, 1998, 2000, 2002, 2004a, 2004b, 2004c) for new product development portfolios. They showed that companies pursue at least one of the three goals of:

- *Maximizing the value of the portfolio.* This aims to maximize the desired objectives of the portfolio and uses various techniques, mainly financial models or scoring models, to identify the parameters for value maximization. The objective is to maximize commercial value of the portfolio at the given resource constraints by, for example, using net present value (NPV) or other measures for Return-on-Investment (ROI). The approach allows for automation of the decision-making processes by, for example, the use of decision support systems that collect required data from the respective organizations, process the data, and prioritize projects, as well as automate the resource allocation process (Iyigün, 1993). Contrary to their popularity, the ROI methods are often criticized for being too number-focused and not taking into account strategic or other non-financial aspects of the business. Some organizations use pre-developed criteria to score and finally rank their projects to identify those of highest priority. These methods lack acceptance, partly due to poorly crafted or outdated criteria, leading to disuse of the models. Cooper et al. (2004b), as well as many other authors, showed that these project selection techniques are associated with low performing portfolios.
- *Achieving the right balance and mix of projects.* Analogous to an investment fund, these portfolios balance risk (or other key parameters) to arrive at the perceived optimum balance of a portfolio. To visualize the result, individual projects are plotted in various grids that show the portfolio's balance in dimensions, such as strategic fit, risk/return, long-term durability, reward, time-to-completion, and competitive impact, among other factors. Similar to the maximization techniques described above, the balance models are criticized for an exaggerated reliance

on financial data and a lack of guidance towards achieving the right balance. In their recent research, Cooper et al. (2004b) showed that these project selection techniques correlate with higher performing portfolios and, thus, are better than those aiming solely for maximization of the portfolio's value.

- *Portfolios for linking strategy with projects.* This approach is concerned with the fit of projects with the organization's strategy. The strategic fit is enforced by either incorporating strategic criteria in the "go/no-go" decisions for projects or allowing funds only for projects aligned with the strategy. It is also known as the *strategic bucket* approach. This method ensures that spending is aligned with the organization's strategy. The technique is criticized for being too time-consuming and somewhat hypothetical, as this process requires splitting resources in the absence of real projects. However, Cooper et al. (2004b) showed that this technique is correlated with highest levels of portfolio performance.

A popular method used to identify projects that do not (or no longer) fit into a portfolio is the one that uses stage gates for project exclusion. This is accomplished by providing an organization's management team with certain sets of information at predetermined stages in projects, so that they can decide on the continuation or cancellation of individual projects. Companies using this method showed higher success rates on launch, sales, and profit of their new products (Cooper et al., 2000).

By comparing high and low performing portfolios, Cooper et al. found that higher performing portfolios include more innovative, riskier, and bolder projects, which are often larger, new-to-the-business, or new-to-the-world projects with high values. High performing portfolios also show a better balance in number of projects and resources available. Companies with high performing portfolios were also found to dedicate more resources to sales and marketing, and to allocate resources based on project merit (Cooper et al., 2004b).

The importance of the right set of projects in a project portfolio for a company's future or market growth over time was identified by Wheelwright and Clark (1992). By looking at a case from the manufacturing sector, they recommend classifying projects by the degree of change in the product and the degree of change in the manufacturing process, which allows classifying portfolios by:

- *Derivative projects*, which are those involving only minor product and process changes
- *Platform projects*, with medium levels of change, and involving the development of the next generation products and processes

- *Breakthrough projects*, with the highest levels of change through new core processes and products
- *R&D projects*, which are outside the commercial project groupings listed above, but develop the *know-how* and *know-why* of new materials and technologies that eventually translate into commercial development.

Wheelwright and Clark (1992) recommend plotting the projects of an organization in a graphical representation of this classification, and then estimating the desired mix of projects by assessing the resource needs and resource capacity; they recommend then deciding on the specific projects to pursue with the existing resources. This helps to determine the type of projects to accept, decline, or eliminate in order to balance the strategic mix and ensure a steady stream of projects in the organization. Furthermore, their approach helps identify the need for future capabilities and development, as it also provides appropriate training and career programs.

By looking at all projects in an organization (not only R&D), Kendall and Rollins (2003) recommend developing portfolios through a three-stage process, which starts by ranking the projects and displaying these by their NPV, risk, internal/external orientation, and originator. The second step involves a ranking by each project's contribution to the sum of benefits from all projects. The third step involves identification of the "strategic resource," which is the primary resource for determining how many projects a company can complete. Finally, they suggest using NPV to identify those projects with the highest return for every workweek of the strategic resource.

In a related approach, Kerzner (2001) recommends graphically displaying the project portfolio in a grid that outlines the project phases and the quality of resources required. A project is displayed as a circle where phase and resource quality needs interconnect. The size of the circle shows the estimated benefits from the project, and a pie chart within the circle shows the percentage of the project that's been completed to date. These techniques identify the projects eligible for the portfolio.

Over the years, a variety of decision-making techniques emerged for project selection. Often developed from operations research, a variety of qualitative or quantitative techniques were developed. Shortcomings with quantitative models include their inadequate handling of multiple evaluation criteria, interrelationships between projects, diversity among projects, as well as insufficient integration of R&D managers' knowledge and experience. Therefore, R&D managers perceive models as difficult to understand and apply (Chien, 2002).

Recent approaches to project selections include that of "real options." Here the (in)-stability of the project's context in the future, and the differences in associated management approaches of the project, influence the application of traditional or more option like approaches to project selection. Often, organizations evaluate the choices between options or, in this case, real options, in a kind of decision tree (Loch & Bode-Greuel, 2001).

A wide variety of selection techniques, tools, methods, and applications is described in detail by Dye and Pennypacker (1999). The book's common theme among 25 papers from different authors is the need to balance quantitative and qualitative information for portfolio decisions, and the need to select portfolio decision criteria depending on the organization's type of portfolio and its strategy. Since an in-depth review of individual techniques lies beyond the scope of this study, interested readers are referred to the book by Dye and Pennypacker (1999) for more information.

An integrated approach to project portfolio selection was developed by Archer and Ghasemzadeh (1999). Based on their review of existing selection techniques, they developed a three-stage process of pre-processing, processing, and post-processing of selection related data; see Figure 3.

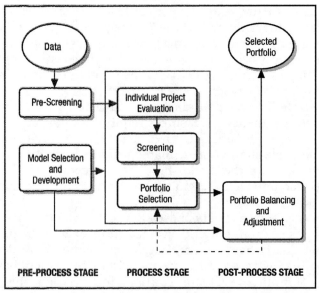

Figure 3    Project Portfolio Selection Process
(Based on Archer & Ghasemzadeh, 1999)

Here, the *pre-processing* stage supports the elimination of infeasible projects, which reduces the workload during the subsequent selection process. During the *processing* stage, data of the individual projects are analyzed and processed into a common form as well as common qualitative and quantitative measures. During *screening*, economic calculations from the previous stage are used to eliminate non-mandatory or other projects that do not meet preset economic criteria. At the *portfolio selection* stage, outputs from the previous stage are combined to select a portfolio based on the objectives of the organization. This often results in a preliminary ranking of the projects based on the objectives specified for the portfolio, and an initial allocation of resources. Sensitivity analysis and other techniques are used to make final adjustments, as well as for balancing of the portfolio. During *portfolio balancing and adjustment*, the decision makers apply judgment to make final adjustments to the portfolio, for example, through use of matrices that graphically display the critical variables of individual projects. *Model selection and development* refers to the initial decision by the organization regarding which techniques to use at each stage of the process. Here, special consideration must be given to the need for a common format for all data, so that appropriate comparisons are possible. The process integrates the most widely used techniques for project selection and should be applicable for a wide range of possible project portfolios.

### Planning and Managing Project Portfolios

Managing portfolios through a joint team of project managers and line managers (as resource owners) is recommended by Platje, Seidel, and Wadman (1994). This portfolio management team uses the individual project plans as input to develop a feasible (re)allocation plan for resources across all projects in the portfolio. Checks and updates of these plans are done regularly. That establishes stability in both the contents and process of the portfolio.

Using examples from several industries, Turner and Speiser (1992) identified the information requirements for portfolio-level planning by showing four different information systems that are needed for synchronized planning at the portfolio, program, and project levels. These four systems are the resource plans, work-package plans, resource schedulers, and team schedulers. Here, work-package plans are passed from the project managers to their portfolio managers for overarching resource planning. Work is then assigned to single disciplines using a resource scheduler, or to multidisciplinary teams using a team scheduler.

A two-level model for portfolio management was developed by Gokhale and Bhatia (1997). Here, the project goals and methodology are fixed for periods of approximately three months, then both are reviewed and, if necessary, revised. This approach allows for the reallocation of resources in the portfolio at the end of each three-month period. Through this approach, the system primarily supports projects with clearly defined objectives and less well-defined methods to achieve these objectives (Turner & Cochrane, 1993).

A scheduling process for projects in a portfolio is shown by Turner (2004). He suggests a six-step process, where:

1. Individual projects are proposed to the portfolio directors.

2. Individual projects are planned by the project managers, and resource requirements are determined.

3. Instead of adding a complete project plan into a giant "plan of plans," each project is added to the portfolio resource plan as a single activity, with idealized resource requirements. This results in a master project schedule.

4. Total resource requirements are compared with resource availability and projects are eliminated until a balance between resource requirements and availability is roughly reached. Then, resource leveling takes place, which might impact the schedule and durations of individual projects.

5. A start date, finish date, and resource profile are determined for all the projects in the portfolio. The projects are then handed over to the project managers for execution within the set window.

6. Project managers then manage the projects and the associated tasks. For this, resources are requested from resource managers, or sometimes work-packages are handed over to resource managers, so that they take on responsibility for the work-package and assign resources to it.

This approach avoids the cumbersome development of a complex "plan of plans" of all projects, which is difficult to develop and maintain.

The managerial problems in business development portfolios were identified by Elonen and Artto (2003). They assessed two portfolios and related their findings to the literature. Through this, they identified six major problem areas:

- Inadequate project-level activities (e.g., through improper implementation of pre-project stages and infrequent progress monitoring)
- Lack of resources, competencies, and methods (e.g., through inadequate methods for portfolio evaluation, lack of resources, or extensive composition of steering groups and teams)
- Lack of commitment, and unclear roles and responsibilities (e.g., at the project level, but also between portfolio managers and other organizations, as well as a lack of management support)

- Inadequate portfolio-level activities (e.g., through overlapping tasks within and among portfolios, weak decision-making, and reluctance to kill projects)
- Inadequate information management regarding information about projects and its flow across the organization
- Inadequate management of project-oriented business (e.g., through low prioritization of projects, lack of project-business strategies, frequently changing roles, responsibilities, and organizational structures).

The study showed the need for more clarity of managers' roles and responsibilities, and the practices for implementation of portfolio management in organizations. It also showed that many of the problems encountered in real-life portfolio work were not addressed in the current literature. Similar to Elonen and Artto (2003), Engwall and Jerbrant (2003) identified problems with project interdependencies, resource allocation, competition of resources, and short-time problem solving. Thus, it shows that a need exists for empirical research into the realities of portfolio management practices.

The last group of portfolio management literature addresses the competencies of project-oriented companies.

### Competencies for Portfolio Management

Competences for the optimization of portfolios were assessed by Gareis (2000), using a multi-method approach. Portfolio coordination and distribution of information material, as well as participation in steering group and project meetings, were found to be important. He also identified program and portfolio management as distinct activities that emerge in organic organizations operated by empowered and process-oriented employees, where portfolio management serves as an integrative function to manage the dynamics of project-oriented companies.

The three aforementioned categories of portfolio management literature show three distinct perspectives, which address different timely stages in portfolio management. The first group addresses the *ex ante* stage, when portfolio definitions are made and projects are selected or rejected for entry in the portfolio. The second group of literature mainly addresses the management techniques needed for planning and managing the portfolio once projects have been assigned—thus, the *ex post* stage of a project's execution in the portfolio. The third category addresses the competency requirements for the two previous groups, and is thereby timely independent.

Even though these differences prevail in the portfolio management literature, the practices described in these groups of literature are not independent of each other. Portfolios do not exist in a vacuum. They are often changed, adapted and refined, to better reflect an organization's strategy or changing market conditions. To that end, the three perspectives are interlinked, as shown in Figure 3. Changes in, for example, the *ex ante* stage impact the practices at the *ex post* stage and possibly influence the competency requirements of the management resources. Portfolios are in a constant flux for the achievement of an organization's objectives.

The next section reviews program management literature.

## Programs and the Management of Programs

Up until the 1990s, considerable confusion about the application of the terms "multi-project management," "program management," and "portfolio management" existed. These terms were often used interchangeably, and program management and portfolio management were often referred to as groups of projects that share some sort of commonality (Pellegrinelli, 1997). In recent years, the literature became more concise and applied terms like "multi-project management" to the management of several smaller and often unrelated projects (Archibald, 2003). Program management is often described as connected with, albeit different from, portfolio management. Projects within programs share a common, overarching objective, and projects in portfolios share the same set of resources (e.g., Lycett, Rassau, & Danson, 2004; Turner & Müller, 2003). The most recent definitions for both management approaches are listed in the introductory chapter of this book.

Program management is often perceived as the top layer of a hierarchy consisting of individual projects (Kerzner, 2001). Program management goals focus on improving efficiency and effectiveness through better prioritization, planning, and coordination in managing projects (Pellegrinelli, 1997), as well as in developing a business focus by defining the goals of individual projects and the entire program regarding requirements, goals, drivers, and culture of the wider organization (Lycett et al., 2004). The literature on program management can be classified into three categories:
- Program management as an entity for organizational structure
- Program management processes and life cycles
- Competencies for program management.

These three categories are described in the following:

### Program Management as an Entity for Organizational Structure

Program management is often described as the next higher organizational hierarchy level above project management. Managers in this function are the intermediaries between higher management and operations personnel, implementing an organization's strategy. Program managers, therefore, link an organization's strategy with the economic implementation through operations. They do this by setting the context for projects and project managers to operate (Pellegrinelli, 2002).

Most of the literature suggests program management to solve problems of linking projects towards a common objective. The approach is, however, also used to address problems of linking projects with their organizational environment. Levene and Braganza (1996), for example, suggest splitting larger business-process re-engineering projects into programs of projects, to overcome the lack of management support and isolation of one-off projects. By implementing planning steps on a rolling-wave basis, the outcomes of projects in a program can be interlinked. With this, a more realistic and feasible plan can be developed.

A continuum of hierarchical management structures for programs is described by Gray (1997). These structures span from loose programs or multi-project groups managed under a single project management umbrella with little control and empowered project managers, up to highly controlled projects that are a function of the project management planning activity and controlled by the program manager and the program stakeholders. Gray suggests choosing a management structure based on the desirability and feasibility of the approach. He suggests that such decisions should be taken on the basis that a management structure is chosen that yields the most beneficial outcome for the program and is, in fact, doable for the organization.

### Program Management Processes and Life Cycles

The processes for project and program management are often described as being similar in nature, albeit different at the detailed level. Both comprise a sequence of steps (e.g., Lycett et al., 2004; PMI, 2003; Thiry, 2004) for initiation or identification, planning or definition, executing, controlling, and closing.

PMI (2003, p. 127) states that these steps are most likely helpful, but not complete explanations of the program management processes. Thiry (2004, p. 252) identifies a program life cycle along a hierarchy of projects, programs, and strategy that is based on:

1. Formulation (sense-making, seeking of alternatives, evaluation of options, and choice)

2. Organization (strategy-planning and selection of actions)

3. Deployment (execution of actions—projects and support, operational activities, and control)

4. Appraisal (assessment of benefits, review of purpose and capability, and re-pacing, if required)

5. Dissolution (reallocation of people and funds, knowledge management, and feedback).

Thiry (2004) describes activities related to the execution stage of a program as assessment and management of the environment and communication, as well as the identification of emerging challenges. This includes a focus on the interdependencies of projects, the program manager's level of intervention in assessing major deliverables, and the output-input relationship of projects in the program, as well as audit and gateway control.

Thiry (2004) defines the activities that occur during the control phase of a program as assessing the need for plan reviews and changes, considering key performance indicators against deliverables, and making decisions to continue, realign, or stop projects.

## Competencies for Program Management

An empirical framework for program management competencies was developed by Pellegrinelli, Partington, and Young (2003) and by Partington, Pellegrinelli, & Young (2005). Their framework consists of four levels of competencies with 17 attributes arranged into three groups of relationships that are then managed. These relationships include *self and the work, self and others*, and *self and program environment*. The four levels represent an increasingly widening view from *focus on details only* to *appreciation of contextual and future consequences*. Lower levels require the understanding of the details and the relationships between activities. The next level works at a summary level, without getting overwhelmed by the details. The third level involves the understanding of the entire program, plus activities that include gaining an understanding of the issues and outcomes for key stakeholders. The highest level holds an overall view of the program and selected details; it appreciates the impact of program decisions and actions outside the program, as well as potential future consequences.

In agreement with other authors, Pellegrinelli et al. (2003) also identified a major difference in the requirements for project managers and program managers. They found that the former should be more focused on strict planning, management, and solving of technical issues, whereas the latter should be increasingly tolerant of uncertainty, more embracing of change, and more aware of the wider business influences. Therefore, program managers need to be better improvisers than implementers of structural approaches (Pellegrinelli, 2002).

This review of program management literature showed three distinct perspectives towards the subject. The first one took an organizational view and looked at the program manager's role in implementing an organization's strategy through programs of projects. The second category looked at the processes needed to manage programs, while the third group identified the underlying competencies required for program management. As in the case of portfolio management, these three categories are not independent, and are linked with each other. Programs and their management are continuously aligned with an organization's strategy and business conditions. Depending on the duration of these programs, these adaptations may vary in pace.

The preceding literature review provides insight into the differences between program and portfolio management concepts. However, it does not provide a clear understanding of the roles and responsibilities of managers working within those frameworks. This understanding will be addressed in the empirical investigation described further on in the report.

## Project Types and Program/Portfolio Management

Differences in project types were investigated, among others, by Shenhar (2001). His popular model uses a two-dimensional matrix of project scope and technological uncertainty to identify different project types with different management requirements.

Turner and Cochrane (1993) identified differences in project type depending on the extent that goals in a project and the methods for achievement of these goals are understood in a project. In a 2 x 2 matrix (as shown in Figure 4), he identifies four different project types, depending on low or high clearness of objectives and methods. Each of these project types requires a different management approach to achieve the project's objectives.

The four different project types are:

**Type 1:** *Projects with well-defined goals and well-defined methods to achieve those goals.* These projects are well understood. It is likely that similar projects were undertaken in the past. The participants will most likely be experts in the technology that is applied within the project. These projects are often engineering projects, such as maintenance projects whose project plans state sequences of well-defined activities.

**Type 2:** *Projects with clearly defined goals, but poorly defined methods.* Here, the functionality of the final product is well understood, but new, and it is not yet known how to best achieve this functionality. These projects are usually product development projects, which are planned in terms of the final deliverables.

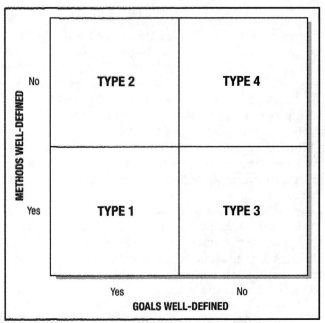

Figure 4      Goals—Methods Matrix (Turner & Cochrane, 1993)

**Type 3:** *Projects with goals that are not clear, but well-defined methods or life-cycles to achieve them.* These projects are often IT application development projects, which are planned in terms of life-cycle stages—where goals are defined in conceptual terms, but their specification is refined through the stages of the project.

**Type 4:** *Projects where neither the objectives nor the methods are known.* What is known is the business problem to be solved or an opportunity to be captured. So the emphasis is on identifying the objectives of a product or service that could solve/capture this problem and then treating it as a Type 2 project. These projects are often organizational change or research projects.

Crawford, Hobbs, and Turner (2004) showed that grouping of projects is an essential step in portfolio management. However, since the categorization purpose for portfolio management is different than it is in project management, the existing systems are rendered inappropriate for portfolio management. The model developed by Crawford et al. (2004) is based on 32 different purposes for classification and 37 attributes to classify projects. While it is more advanced in terms of applicability to program and portfolio management, the system does not outline the relationship between project groups/

classifications and the associated portfolio management practices, roles, and responsibilities.

## Environmental Complexity

The axiom that organizations adopt different management styles to meet the situational demands of their environment is one of the traditional themes in management literature. The concept is based on Contingency Theory, which claims that the characteristics of leadership and the situational requirements must match in order to produce the best possible results for an organization (Burns & Stalker, 1961). More recent developments in this field indicate that organizations often operate in several markets in parallel (such as national and international, or product development and organizational change projects) and, therefore, are required to match several environments simultaneously. Traditional bivariate contingency relationships, therefore, are seen as being too static to reflect organizations' dynamics (Galunic & Eisenhardt, 1994). Research suggests that dynamic environments require experiential product development using frequent iterations, testing, and milestones (Brown & Eisenhardt, 1995). Environments, therefore, can be modeled on a simple-to-complex continuum, with simple being a well-understood environment for which reliable, effective ways of dealing exist. Complex environments are poorly understood, and reliable, effective ways of dealing with the environment are not known to the organization. The extent of change in the factors representing the environment is defined as its stability. This stability ranges from stable to turbulent (or dynamic) environments (Pethis & Saias, 1978).

A study by Bettis and Hall (1981) indicated that portfolio management is mainly used either by diversified firms that use portfolio planning techniques to aggregate business for strategic analysis and repositioning, or by dominant, vertical firms to guide diversity away from low-growth sectors. By assessing corporate results, the study indicates that companies using portfolio management better fit their environment. After implementing portfolio management, two out of the three firms assessed in the study substantially improved their market position relative to their competitors. The use of portfolio management was mostly triggered by poor financial performance and the perception that strategic issues were not surfacing.

In summary, the underlying organizational approaches and distinctions in roles between line and project management (such as line, project, program, and portfolio managers) are not yet understood and require further investigation (Brown & Eisenhardt, 1995).

The review of literature indicates a relationship between environmental complexity and the use of organizational approaches, such as program and portfolio management.
This forms research hypothesis 1 (H1):

> *H1: An organization's perceived environmental complexity is directly related to the use of program and portfolio management practices.*

The review of project types shows a contingency between project type and project management approach. With programs and portfolios representing a higher-level dimension of project management, it can be hypothesized that these contingencies are also reflected at the program and portfolio level. Therefore, research hypothesis 2 reads:

> *H2: Different project types are correlated with different program and portfolio management roles and responsibilities.*

Research hypotheses 3 and 4 are derived from the results of the aforementioned Bettis and Hall (1981) study, with H3 addressing the depth of program and portfolio management implementation in the organization, and H4 addressing the different roles and responsibilities associated with it:

> *H3: Governance practices in program and portfolio management differ significantly between high- and low-performing organizations.*

> *H4: Middle managers' roles and responsibilities in program and portfolio management differ significantly between high- and low-performing organizations.*

Research assesses the practices, roles, and responsibilities of middle managers in program and portfolio management, as well as the impact of project type and an organization's environmental complexity on these practices, roles and responsibilities. The variables for project type and organizational environment are classified as independent variables. Program and portfolio management practices, roles and responsibilities are classified as dependent variables. The high-level research model is shown in Figure 5.

The results will be structured by low- and high-performing organizations. This allows drawing theoretical conclusions, as well as identifying "best-practices."

The study's methodology is described in the next chapter.

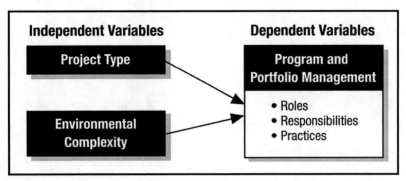

Figure 5     High-Level Research Model

# CHAPTER 3

# Methodology and Analysis

A sequential multi-method approach was used to obtain the highest levels of generalizability and credibility of results (McGrath, 1982). This methodological approach was chosen for balancing the inherent flaws in reliability and validity of the measurement constructs of each of the individual methods (McGrath 1982, Remenyi, Williams, Money, & Swartz, 1998). A combination of several methods and triangulation of their results allows for more confidence in the research results (Jick, 1979).

Execution of the research model started with an exploratory qualitative study to develop a basic understanding of the roles and responsibilities under the two governance structures. Following that, a quantitative study was performed to confirm the findings and test the hypotheses. This order (qualitative followed by quantitative) is also used for the report in this chapter.

## The Qualitative Study

The approach followed Yin's (1994) methodology for case-study research. Using a grounded theory approach (Glaser & Strauss, 1967), the roles and responsibilities of the two groups of managers were identified through a continuous comparison of interview results. The simultaneous work of data collection and analysis were guided by the questions "How do project type and organizational complexity determine the use of project portfolio and program management in organizations?" and "What are middle managers' practices, roles and responsibilities in program and portfolio management in successful organizations?"

The qualitative study was based on the assumption that new data, new cases, and—in this study—new interviews would create new knowledge and improved understanding, in order to answer the research questions. Empirical data on managerial actions, collected through interviews, were used to identify the roles and responsibilities of middle managers. Data were immediately analyzed after each interview and subsequently interpreted. This was done through constant comparison of the newly collected data with existing data, and the coding from previous interviews. A systematic coding started with first-level codes or terms used by the managers interviewed. Through iterative analyses, the first-level codes were refined into general codes, following Strauss and Corbin (1988, p. 212), until:

> (a) no new or relevant data seem to be emerging regarding a category, (b) the category is well developed in terms of its properties and dimensions demonstrating variation, and (c) the relationships among categories are well established and validated.

This process allowed:

1. Focusing data collection activities and improving *theoretical sampling* (Glaser & Strauss, 1967).

2. Identifying patterns, and achieving *theoretical saturation* in these patterns.

The importance of theoretical saturation for the developed theory and its validity cannot be underestimated. Pattern-matching techniques (Miles & Huberman, 1994), therefore, were used to identify typical program and portfolio management-related practices, roles, and responsibilities of the managers. NVIVO software was used for the analysis of qualitative data, and for keeping track of codes and emerging patterns. These patterns were later used as concepts for the development of questionnaire items for the quantitative study.

A series of 9 semi-structured interviews were held with 11 managers in 5 different industries and 5 different countries. Respondents were selected based on the importance of their organization in a particular industry or geographical area. Annual turnover of the firms ranged from US$160 million to US$8.8 billion in 2003. The interviews were held either face-to-face or through conference calls and were tape-recorded for subsequent analysis. Six of the interviewees held positions as vice president, business unit director, or department manager, and five were in program and portfolio management roles. Details about geography, industry, company type, roles, and titles can be found in Table 2.

Interviewees held a wide variety of organizational titles (see Table 2). In many cases, their title did not directly identify them as a program or portfolio manager, even though they performed such tasks. During the analysis, interviewees were classified as a program or portfolio manager based on the individuals' tasks in their organiza-

| Industry | Type of Company | Country of Interviewee | Title of Interviewee |
|---|---|---|---|
| Biotechnology | R & D in plant breeding and plant biotechnology | Germany | Senior Consultant, Portfolio Management |
| Construction | Facilities networking | Sweden | Director, Project Management Office |
| Construction | Railway construction | Sweden | Project Manager |
| Food | Processing and packaging | Sweden | Program Manager, Portfolio Manager, Head of Business Unit |
| Information Systems | IT services and consulting | USA | Director of Program Management |
| Information Systems | IT services and consulting | USA | Director, Program Management R&D |
| Information Systems | IT services and consulting | Australia | Vice President |
| Information Systems | IT Systems development and maintenance | Denmark | Department Manager |
| Telecom | Consulting | Sweden | Senior Consultant, Program/Portfolio Management |

Table 2    Industry, Company, Country, and Role of
           Interviewees

tion. An example is a project manager for a five-year, US$430 million railway construction project that included more than 25 larger sub-projects. This interviewee's responses were grouped under "program manager" due to the complexity of the undertaking (the larger project was comprised of several larger and smaller projects). Another example is a department manager who ran several projects simultaneously to develop and maintain a client's IT system. This individual's task included many projects over an extended period of time, but the number and duration of projects was less than those of the manager involved in the railroad project. In the department manager example, the two roles of program manager and portfolio manager were intertwined. The person's activities were sorted according to the profile of either program manager or portfolio manager. Generally, the interviewees' activities (the *what* and *how* of their work) classified their role. The criteria used by their managers to evaluate each interviewee's program or portfolio were classified as each interviewee's responsibility.

### Qualitative Data Analysis Results

Managers with portfolio management roles are found at medium or higher levels in the organizational hierarchy, typically as director or vice president. The common responsibility that middle managers share in portfolio management is the leveling of resources across projects, with the objective of maximizing the economic use of resources within a portfolio. Furthermore, they are often responsible for achieving financial objectives in managing their portfolio (e.g., by lowering the negative financial impact of troubled projects). Through their responsibilities, which include achieving financial results in relation to the annual business plan, they become indirectly accountable for shareholder value. Even though traditional project performance indicators for projects within a portfolio are important for the middle managers in managing their portfolio of projects, these indicators are often dealt with or delegated to program managers and project managers. Tools that these managers use include aggregated red/yellow/green status reports of the projects, organizational time and cost information from corporate ERP systems, profit and loss statements, and short- and long-term corporate strategic plans.

Those managers with a stronger focus on the program management role aim for maximizing the results of their particular program. Managers performing both roles simultaneously aim for a balance between the short-term goals of the program and the long-term goals of the portfolio.

Middle managers with roles in program management are typically found at a lower or medium level of management, such as department manager or director. Related responsibilities include creation of stakeholder value through achievement of a program's time and budget objectives, as well as delivery of contracted products or services. Their focus is mainly on the timely delivery of programs. Responsibility for quality is often delegated to the project managers. The tools they use include aggregated project information, resource databases for skills per person and people per project, and databases of possible subcontractors for projects.

The managers' program and portfolio management roles are performed before and after a single project or program is started. These roles fall into three categories addressing effectiveness, coordination, and efficiency of program and portfolio management. Table 3 shows the categories and roles.

Prior to project execution, managers aim for effectiveness, or *selection of the right projects*, by identifying, assessing, selecting, and planning for appropriate business opportunities. This is often done by evaluating business opportunities against a set of predetermined selection criteria, such as profit margins, strategic value of

| | Effectiveness | Coordination | Efficiency |
|---|---|---|---|
| Portfolio management roles prior to project execution | • Business planning<br>• Project selection | • Resource procurement | • Project / program plan review |
| Program management roles prior to project execution | • Identification of business opportunities | • Synergy identification<br>• Resource selection | |
| Both roles during project execution | • Identification of bad projects | • Resource planning<br>• Participation in steering groups<br>• Prioritization of projects[a]<br>• Coordination of projects[b]<br>• Collection and aggregation of reports | • Initiate[a] / conduct[b] reviews<br>• Handling of issues<br>• Coaching of project managers<br>• Improvement of processes |

[a] = mainly in portfolio management role
[b] = mainly in program management role

**Table 3    Framework of Program and Portfolio Management Roles of Middle Managers**

customer delivery projects, or Return on Investment (ROI) in organizations' internal projects. Coordination takes place through resource planning and procurement, as well as identification of synergies between projects. Efficiency is achieved through project/program plan reviews and selection of the right resources. This ensures that organizations execute their projects at the *lowest possible cost.*

During project execution, both the program and portfolio management roles include:

- Identification of bad projects for increased efficiency, participation in steering groups, coordination and prioritization of projects, collection and aggregation of reports for coordination of projects
- Project reviews, coaching, issue handling, and improvement of corporate processes for increased efficiency in execution.

Even though the program and portfolio management roles are similar during project execution, they differ slightly in extent due to their differences in a program or portfolio management context.

The roles identified during this study (and shown in Table 3) were subsequently validated through a quantitative study, which is described in the following section. The individual roles are further explained in Chapter 4: *Managerial Implications: What Middle Managers in Successful Organizations Do.*

## The Quantitative Study

The research model was executed through the combination of a qualitative study and a quantitative study, with the former identifying the roles and responsibilities of middle managers in program and portfolio management, and the latter confirming the results. This quantitative study also investigated the impact of environmental complexity and project type on program and portfolio management roles, responsibilities and practices of middle managers. The quantitative analysis was performed in three steps:

1. Validating the results from the qualitative study.

2. Assessing the correlation between independent variables and dependent variables.

3. Modeling the relationship of roles and practices with environment and project type.

The independent variables of the research model were operationalized using 5-point Likert scales for the following constructs:

- *Project type* was assessed through a series of project attributes, which were subsequently factor-analyzed to identify the respondents' underlying project type structures
- *Environmental complexity* was assessed by using the popular set of questions developed by Duncan (1972). Here, two dimensions of complexity are assessed. The simple/complex dimension measures the number and similarity of environmental factors taken into account during decision-making in organizations. A high level indicates a complex decision-making process due to a large number of factors that need to be taken into account. The static/dynamic dimension indicates the degree to which the factors for decision-making are the same over time or continually change. A high level indicates a frequent change in factors.

Dependent variables of the research model were operationalized through the concepts of:

- *Governance practices*, as a set of questions that measure the extent to which an organization uses program and portfolio management techniques, tools, and associated processes. This includes project prioritization, selection of projects depending on the organization's strategy, prioritization of projects, communication of portfolio results, use of similar metrics to measure results, use of steering groups and a group decision-making style (versus individual decisions), the extent of face-to-face meetings, and the extent that decisions are made in the best interest of the organization. All measures were taken on 5-point Likert scales. The questions were subsequently factor analyzed to identify the underlying structures for practices in program and portfolio management.

- *Roles*, a set of questions derived from the roles identified in the qualitative study. These were also measured on 5-point Likert scales.
- *Responsibilities*, a set of yes/no questions that assessed the respondents' responsibilities, as identified and described in the foregoing qualitative study.

A set of questions, based on (Duncan, 1972), was developed to assess the TCE dimensions of product uniqueness and risk. Responses, however, showed more than 80% of missing values for these questions. This set of questions, therefore, was not used for analysis.

A Web-based questionnaire was used to collect data. After a pretest, an introduction letter and the Web-link were e-mailed to chapter representatives of professional organizations for managers and program/portfolio managers. They were asked to forward the survey to their members or other managers working with program and portfolio management. Quality in the responses was ensured by having the survey sent only to professionals. Organizations addressed included the Institute of Directors, IEEE Engineering Management, IEEE Computer Society, IEEE Aerospace, The Swedish Project Management Society, PMO Interest Group of Sweden, National Association of Corporate Directors; Society for Human Resource Management, The Performance Measurement Association, as well as Project Management Institute (PMI) and International Project Management Association (IPMA). The sampling resulted in a convenience sample, whose sample frame and traditional response rate could not be calculated due to the snowball approach that was used.

### Sample Demographics

The number of responses totaled 244, of which 242 were used for analysis. Two respondents were excluded because of unrealistic responses. Seventy-four persons (31%) were under 40 years of age, 102 persons (42%) were between 41-50 years, and 65 persons (27%) were above 51 years old. The mean age was 45.5 years. See Table 4.

Average business experience was 20 years. Thirty-eight percent had up to 15 years of business experience, 36% had between 16 and 25 years, and 26% had more than 25 years of business experience. The details are in Table 5.

| | | Frequency | Percent | Valid Percent | Cumulative Percent |
|---|---|---|---|---|---|
| Valid | −30 | 5 | 2.1 | 2.1 | 2.1 |
| | 31–40 | 69 | 28.5 | 28.6 | 30.7 |
| | 41–50 | 102 | 42.1 | 42.3 | 73.0 |
| | 51–60 | 51 | 21.1 | 21.2 | 94.2 |
| | 61– | 14 | 5.8 | 5.8 | 100.0 |
| | Total | 241 | 99.6 | 100.0 | |
| Missing | System | 1 | .4 | | |
| Total | | 242 | 100.0 | | |

Table 4    Quantitative Study Demographics: Age

| | | Frequency | Percent | Valid Percent | Cumulative Percent |
|---|---|---|---|---|---|
| Valid | −5 | 13 | 5.4 | 5.4 | 5.4 |
| | 6–15 | 78 | 32.2 | 32.2 | 37.6 |
| | 16–25 | 87 | 36.0 | 36.0 | 73.6 |
| | 26–35 | 46 | 19.0 | 19.0 | 92.6 |
| | 36– | 18 | 7.4 | 7.4 | 100.0 |
| | Total | 242 | 100.0 | 100.0 | |

Table 5    Quantitative Study Demographics: Years of Business Experience

Mean current position experience was 4 years. Twenty-four percent had one year or less experience in their current position, while 45% had more than four years experience. Fifty-six percent were certified project managers. Details can be found in Table 6.

| | | Frequency | Percent | Valid Percent | Cumulative Percent |
|---|---|---|---|---|---|
| Valid | 0–1 | 57 | 23.6 | 23.6 | 23.6 |
| | 2–3 | 77 | 31.8 | 31.8 | 55.4 |
| | 4–5 | 51 | 21.1 | 21.1 | 76.4 |
| | 6–10 | 44 | 18.2 | 18.2 | 94.6 |
| | 11– | 13 | 5.4 | 5.4 | 100.0 |
| | Total | 242 | 100.0 | 100.0 | |

Table 6    Quantitative Study Demographics: Years in Current Position

|         |                      | Frequency | Percent | Valid Percent | Cumulative Percent |
|---------|----------------------|-----------|---------|---------------|--------------------|
| Valid   | North America        | 97        | 40.1    | 40.4          | 40.4               |
|         | Scandinavian counties| 78        | 32.2    | 32.5          | 72.9               |
|         | Other parts of Europe| 40        | 16.5    | 16.7          | 89.6               |
|         | Other parts the world| 25        | 10.3    | 10.4          | 100.0              |
|         | **Total**            | **240**   | **99.2**| **100.0**     |                    |
| Missing | System               | 2         | .8      |               |                    |
|         | **Total**            | **242**   | **100.0**|              |                    |

Table 7    Quantitative Study Demographics: Geographic
           Dispersion

As shown in Table 7, the respondents were from 26 countries, including 40% from North America, 32% from the Scandinavian countries (Denmark, Finland, Norway, and Sweden), nearly 17% from other parts of Europe, and 10% from other parts of the world. Sixty-five percent worked with projects internal to their organization, and 35% with external projects.

Forty-six percent of the respondents indicated that they are working in program or portfolio management, while 51% indicated they work as other managers or consultants. ANOVA analysis of the differences between responses showed no significant differences between the two groups (at $p = .05$). All responses, therefore, were used for the subsequent analyses.

Demographic dispersion by industry showed a dominance of respondents from the IT industry (37%), followed by Engineering (27%) and Services (25%). Education and other industries were both below 4% of the responses. Details are shown in Table 8.

|       |             | Frequency | Percent | Valid Percent | Cumulative Percent |
|-------|-------------|-----------|---------|---------------|--------------------|
| Valid | IS/IT       | 90        | 37.2    | 37.2          | 37.2               |
|       | Engineering | 65        | 26.9    | 26.9          | 64.0               |
|       | Services    | 61        | 25.2    | 25.2          | 89.3               |
|       | Government  | 12        | 5.0     | 5.0           | 94.2               |
|       | Education   | 5         | 2.1     | 2.1           | 96.3               |
|       | Other       | 9         | 3.7     | 3.7           | 100.0              |
|       | **Total**   | **242**   | **100.0**| **100.0**    |                    |

Table 8    Quantitative Study Demographics: Industries

## Quantitative Data Analysis Results

Step 1 of the analysis started by validating questionnaire constructs for the six types of roles (see Table 2), as well as the responsibilities and governance practices.

Cronbach Alpha values between .73 and .80 showed acceptable reliability levels for the questions on *roles*. Averages were taken for each construct, resulting in the following role-related variables:

- *bus_plg:* identification of business opportunities and business planning
- *bproj_id:* involvement in identification of bad projects
- *res_plg:* involvement in resource planning and procurement
- *adm_wk:* involvement in steering groups, prioritization and coordination of projects, collection and aggregation of reports
- *iss_wk:* involvement in reviews, handling of issues, coaching of project managers, and general improvement of organization-wide processes
- *pln_rev:* involvement in reviews of program and project plans.

*Responsibility*-related dependent variables (ordinal) were:

- *act_pln:* accountability for the achievement of annual business plans
- *act_pgm:* accountability for the achievement of planned projects and programs
- *rsp_sha:* shared responsibilities between peer-level managers
- *rep_sta:* a position that staff reports to
- *rep_pm:* a position that project managers report to

*Governance practices* for program and portfolio management were assessed through a set of reliable questions ($\alpha = .86$). Factor analysis was used to reduce the number of variables. The extracted factor variables were used as replacements for the original variables in subsequent analyses.

Two underlying governance dimensions were identified:

- *pra_tech:* application of dedicated processes, techniques, and tools for program and portfolio management, such as those listed above
- *pra_dec:* decision-making practices, as listed above.

This confirmed the usability of the constructs for measurement of the dependent variables.

Step 2 of the analysis started by identifying the independent variables.

Factor analysis of the variables for *project type* identified the respondents by distinguishing between:

- *pt_prod:* product-related projects
- *pt_org:* organizational change-related projects
- *pt_time:* longer-term projects (> 1 year, > 3 years).

*Organizational complexity* was calculated as described by Duncan (1972), resulting in two independent variables for:

- *complexity:* number of factors taken into account during decision-making
- *dynamic:* frequency of change in factors for decision-making.

Performance of the organization was assessed through nine questions using 5-point Likert scales to measure an organization's success in projects, programs and portfolios ($\alpha = .84$). The results were averaged for an overall performance measure of the organization. This scale variable was subsequently converted to ordinal for classification of organizations by their performance level (variable: *lohi_perf*). Organizations at or above the sample mean were classified as high performing (coded 1), and those under the sample mean as low performing (coded 0).

Figure 6 shows the detailed research model together with the associated variables, as previously described. The model allows for assessments of correlation between all independent and dependent variables.

The research hypotheses were tested through regression and correlation analyses. Statistical significance was assessed at the .05 level, and practical significance through effect size, which is *"the estimate of the magnitude to which a phenomena being studied exists in the population"* (Hair, Anderson, Tatham, & Black, 1998, p. 2). Classification of effect sizes was done through the regressions' $R^2$, with thresholds for small effect size at $R^2$ of .02, medium at .13, and large at .26 (Cohen 1988, p. 413).

- Correlation between independent variables and responsibility variables was tested using Spearman correlations. No correlations were found.
- Correlation of governance and roles variables was tested through a stepwise regression analysis of governance practices and roles variables against all independent variables.

The results are shown in Table 9

Environmental complexity is positively correlated with governance practices using advanced techniques, tools, and processes ($p < .001$). An $R^2$ of .314 indicates high practical significance through a very large effect size. This confirms research hypothesis H1. Organizations' perceived environmental complexity is directly related to the use of program and portfolio management as governance practice.

The positive correlation between environmental complexity and the roles for business planning and issue handling indicates the emergence of these roles in organizations where decision-making is complex due to a large number of factors that need to be taken into account. The frequency of change in these factors, as well as the

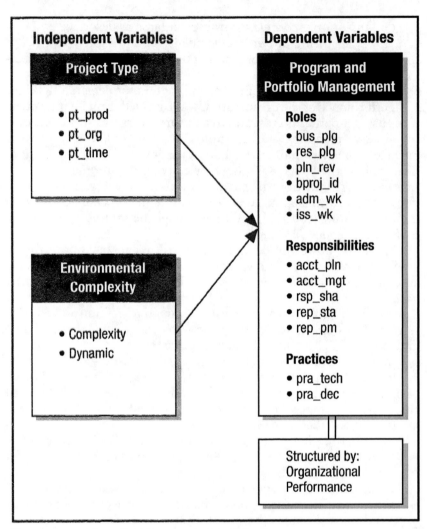

Figure 6    Detailed Research Model

extent of product content in a program, does not seem to impact governance practices or roles.

The organizational change content in projects positively correlates with the emergence of roles for resource planning, administrative work, and issue handling. This indicates an increase in coordination activities through these types of projects. The duration of projects is positively related to the roles for business planning, project/program plan reviews, and bad project identification. This shows increased sensitivity for effectiveness and efficiency in longer-

| | Governance practices | | Roles | | | | | | Responsibilities | | | | |
| | pra_tech | pra_dec | bus_plg | res_plg | pln_rev | bproj_id | adm_wk | iss_wk | act_pln | act_pgm | rsp_sha | rep_sta | rep_pm |
|---|---|---|---|---|---|---|---|---|---|---|---|---|---|
| *Independent Variables* | | | | | | | | | | | | | |
| Complexity | +**** | 0 | +*** | 0 | 0 | 0 | 0 | +*** | 0 | 0 | 0 | 0 | 0 |
| Dynamic | 0 | 0 | 0 | 0 | 0 | 0 | 0 | 0 | 0 | 0 | 0 | 0 | 0 |
| pt_prod | 0 | 0 | 0 | +** | 0 | 0 | 0 | 0 | 0 | 0 | 0 | 0 | 0 |
| pt_org | 0 | 0 | +**** | 0 | 0 | 0 | +* | +*** | 0 | 0 | 0 | 0 | 0 |
| pt_time | 0 | 0 | +**** | 0 | +* | +** | 0 | 0 | 0 | 0 | 0 | 0 | 0 |
| LoHi Performance | +**** | 0 | 0 | 0 | 0 | +** | 0 | 0 | 0 | 0 | 0 | 0 | –* |
| $R^2$ | .314 | | .075 | .036 | .022 | .045 | .021 | .059 | | | | | |

Note: 0 = not significant   +/– = significant positive or negative correlation

*Significant at $p < .05$
**Significant at $p < .01$
***Significant at $p < .005$
****Significant at $p < .001$
n = 242

**Table 9**   Correlations between Independent and Dependent Variables

term projects. All *roles*-related correlations show practical significance, albeit with small effect sizes. This partly confirms research hypothesis H2. Different project types are correlated with different program and portfolio management roles, but not with responsibilities.

Significant differences between low and high performing organizations were found in governance practices using advanced techniques, tools and processes, as well as in the role for identification of bad projects in organizations. Higher performing organizations scored significantly higher on these two factors (p = .05). That confirms research hypothesis H3. Governance practices in program and portfolio management differ significantly between high and low performing organizations.

Analysis of differences of responsibilities in low and high performing organizations was done using ANOVA. A significant difference was found in responsibility for project managers. In low performing companies, project managers often report to middle managers, whereas in high performing companies, project managers report elsewhere. This confirms, albeit weakly, research hypothesis H4. Middle managers' responsibilities in program and portfolio management differ significantly between high and low performing organizations.

The extent of business planning was also identified as being significantly higher in high performing organizations.

Step 3 of the analysis was done to identify patterns of program and portfolio management roles in different situations. Canonical correlation analysis was used for modeling the relationship between the group of independent variables and the group of dependent variables in different situational contexts. Canonical loadings were used for interpretation of the models, which allow for interpretation of the results as factors. The usual .3 threshold for significance of loadings was applied (Hair et al., 1998). Two models were found, one statistically significant at .05, and one just above the statistical threshold for insignificance (p = .056).

Across all responses, the combination of environmental complexity, organizational change content of projects, and the duration of projects is correlated with all roles (see Model 1 in Table 10). It identifies the importance of all roles for balancing the "soft" organizational factors and the "hard" time factors in business.

This is also depicted in Figure 7, which shows the canonical correlation model graphically, placing the independent variables for environmental turbulence and project types in the upper part, and the correlated dependent variables for roles in the lower part. The clustering of the variables at one side of the continuum shows the integration of roles, project type, and environment. This identifies

| | Model 1:<br>All respondents | Model 2:<br>Low performing<br>organizations |
|---|---|---|
| Complexity | **−0.751** | **0.525** |
| Dynamic | −0.001 | 0.107 |
| pt_prod | 0.107 | **0.362** |
| pt_org | **−0.355** | **−0.701** |
| pt_time | **−0.599** | **0.471** |
| bus_plg | **−0.923** | 0.174 |
| res_plg | **−0.497** | **−0.429** |
| pln_rev | **−0.580** | 0.194 |
| bprj_id | **−0.646** | 0.159 |
| adm_wk | **−0.589** | **−0.516** |
| iss_wk | **−0.695** | 0.003 |
| Sign. | 0.041 | 0.059 |
| Wilk's | 0.797 | 0.573 |
| Chi-Square | 44.757 | 42.936 |
| DF | 30.000 | 30.000 |
| Canonical Correlations | 0.328 | 0.435 |
| Redundancy Index | 0.048 | 0.017 |
| n | 242 | 101 |

Note: significant loadings are shown in bold

Table 10     Canonical Correlation Models

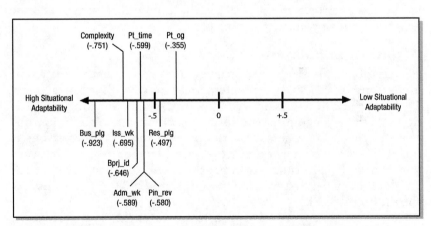

Figure 7     Canonical Correlation Model (All Responses)

a high adaptability of an organization's roles to their situation (i.e., environment and project type).

Model 2, even though it's at the borderline of insignificance, shows that low performing organizations balance the requirements from the organizational parts of their projects through resource plan-

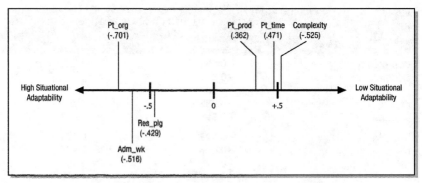

Figure 8    Canonical Correlation Model (Low Performing
            Organizations Only)

ning and administrative work. This is also done by other organizations (see Model 1). However, low performing companies do not balance the requirements stemming from the environmental complexity, as well as product contents and duration of projects through any of the roles. This is depicted in Figure 8. Three of the four situational variables are disconnected from the rest and no roles are in place to handle the requirements arising from these environmental factors. It is indicated that middle managers in these organizations ignore the environment, as well as the importance of product and time for their organizations' projects.

## Results Triangulation

The results of the study were triangulated with those identified by Elonen and Artto (2003) as problem areas for portfolio management. To do so, the differences between low and high performing organizations in their program/portfolio management practices, roles, and project types were assessed on the level of individual questions of the questionnaire. Answers significantly different ($p < .05$) between low and high performing organizations were mapped against the problem areas defined by Elonen and Artto (2003). The results are shown in Table 11.

It shows that roles used to a lesser extent in low performing organizations match the problem areas of inadequate project level activities; lack of resources, competence and methods; as well as lack of commitment, unclear roles and responsibilities. Practices underrepresented in low performing organizations matched against the areas of inadequate activities at the portfolio level, information management, and inadequate management of the project-oriented business.

Findings not identified by Elonen and Artto (2003) are the particular performance improvements through program and portfolio management practices in organizations running projects with a high service and organizational change content, and delivery to external organizations. That identifies program and portfolio management as especially appropriate for delivery projects in buyer-seller relationships.

| | Inadequate project level activities | Lack of resources, competencies and methods | Lack of commitment, unclear roles, and responsibilities | Inadequate portfolio level activities | Inadequate information management | Inadequate management of project-oriented business |
|---|---|---|---|---|---|---|
| **The middle manager is ...** | | | | | | |
| -involved in resource procurement | X | X | | | | |
| -involved in identification of bad projects | X | | | | | X |
| -working in steering groups | X | X | X | | | |
| -involved in project and project group reviews | X | X | X | | | |
| -involved in handling issues related to projects | X | | X | | | |
| **The organization ...** | | | | | | |
| -prioritizes projects | | | | X | | |
| -selects projects on the basis of the organization's strategy | | | | | | X |
| -communicates which projects are important | | | | | X | |
| -uses a tool to collect and disseminate information about the status of all high priority projects | | | | | X | |
| -all reporting to steering committee is done using the same templates | | | | | X | |
| -uses similar metrics for reporting similar projects | | | | | X | |
| -decisions about groups of projects are made as joint management decisions | | | | | | X |
| -decisions about groups of projects are made in the best interest of the company | | | | | | X |
| -facilitates effective management of the work in order to meet strategic annual business objectives (uses portfolio management) | | | | | | X |
| -portfolios are managed by a single manager or group of manager | | | | X | | |
| -groups projects together to obtain benefits and control not available from managing them individually | | | | | | X |
| Project deliverables are services | | | | | | |
| Projects aim to develop our own or a client's organization | | | | | | |
| Projects aim to deliver a result to another firm or institution | | | | | | |

Roles · Practices · Project type

Elonen & Artto (2003) defined problem areas

Areas low performing organizations scored significantly lower

Table 11    Mapping Study Results against Elonen & Artto (2003) Results

# CHAPTER 4

# Managerial Implications: What Middle Managers in Successful Organizations Do

This chapter is a discussion and summary of the findings from the Methodology and Analysis chapter. It shows how high performing organizations structure themselves to handle the complexity stemming from their own organization, their types of projects, and their clients' requirements. The chapter starts from a broad, organizational-wide perspective and shows the breadth and depth with which high performing organizations implement program and portfolio management practices. Then, the perspective changes towards the activities of middle managers in these organizations. Finally, the framework for roles and responsibilities, developed in the previous chapter, is discussed in detail and reconciled with existing practices described in the literature. Suggestions for further literature are provided for interested readers. The chapter ends with a set of practical recommendations for implementing program and portfolio management.

## Organizing for Program and Portfolio Management

Organizations in the study adopted one of four possible governance structures:
- Neither program nor portfolio management
- Program management only
- Program and portfolio management (hybrid)
- Portfolio management only.

Assessment of organizational performance by governance structure showed that hybrid structures perform significantly better (p < .05) than all other governance structures.

Those organizations using neither program nor portfolio management perform lowest, while those using either program or portfolio

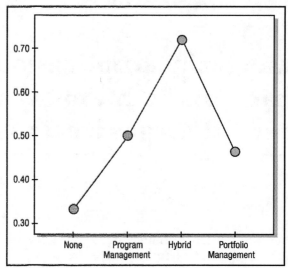

Figure 9    Organizational Performance in Different Governance Structures

management perform slightly (but not significantly) better. Figure 9 shows the relative performance of organizations in different governance structures. Statistical details, as well as details on average performance of projects, programs, and portfolios in different governance structures are provided in Table 16 and 17, as well as Figure 13 in Appendix C.

This is supported by the Canonical Correlation Models developed in the Methodology and Analysis chapter. These models showed that organizations' differences in performance are related to their ability to adapt to changing situations. Higher performing organizations are able to balance the variety of requirements, both internal and external, through appropriate roles in the organization. Low performing organizations focus too much on their internal administration and are lacking roles to appropriately address, for example, the specific technology and time requirements stemming from their project types. Furthermore, they are lacking roles for dealing with the organization's environmental complexity, which includes managing the internal stakeholders and decision-makers.

These issues are addressed through program and portfolio management roles. Program management roles executed by middle managers ensure a cohesive set of requirements stemming from a common (program) objective. It moves the program (with all its projects) in the center of the organization's activities. That provides a vision for the organization and shifts priorities away from internal (administrative) tasks to external customer delivery tasks. It builds awareness for the organization's primary reason for existence: to deliver value to its customers.

Portfolio management roles executed by middle managers balance the organization's environmental complexity through clearly defined processes and criteria for project selection, as well as decision-making authorities. Such workflow:

- Simplifies decision-making processes
- Identifies and eliminates projects and tasks not related to the organization's strategy
- Allows project and program managers to focus on their delivery tasks.

The combination of program and portfolio management roles, therefore, maximizes effectiveness and efficiency of the organization's operation.

### Managers' Activities in Program and Portfolio Management

Based on the qualitative study, a number of roles were identified. As shown in Table 12, managers devote most of their time to the handling of project-related issues, followed by plan reviews and improvement of processes. The least time is spent on resource procurement and identifications of bad projects.

Differences in the amount of time managers spent in their different program and portfolio management roles were found between high and low performing organizations. Managers in high performing organizations devote more time than managers in low performing organizations to:

- Handling of project-related issues
- Review of projects
- Work in steering groups
- Procurement of resources
- Identification of bad projects.

Priorities seem to differ slightly between some activities. Managers in low performing organizations put nearly as much time into improving internal processes as do their counterparts in high performing organizations. However, they spent much less time on reviews of projects and groups of projects, as depicted in Table 13.

| | N | Mean | Std. Deviation |
|---|---|---|---|
| I am involved in handling issues related to projects or groups of projects | 239 | 3.47 | 1.068 |
| Before work on project deliverables begins I am involved in project plan reviews | 241 | 3.26 | 1.077 |
| I am involved in the improvement of my firm's or institution's internal processes | 242 | 3.26 | 1.071 |
| I am involved in resource planning | 239 | 3.19 | 1.139 |
| I am involved in the coordination of projects to achieve time, cost or resources efficiency | 241 | 3.11 | 1.142 |
| I am involved in reviews of projects or groups of projects | 240 | 3.05 | 1.179 |
| I am involved in business planning for the projects that the organization I manage is involved in | 241 | 2.98 | 1.167 |
| I coach or mentor project managers | 241 | 2.91 | 1.244 |
| I collect reports from projects | 240 | 2.89 | 1.214 |
| I am involved in identifying business opportunities | 241 | 2.75 | 1.196 |
| I am involved in the prioritization of projects | 241 | 2.75 | 1.200 |
| I am working in steering groups for projects or groups of projects | 241 | 2.63 | 1.282 |
| I am involved in resource procurement | 241 | 2.61 | 1.149 |
| I am involved in identification of bad projects in the organization | 242 | 2.46 | 1.181 |

Table 12    Managers' Time Spent on Different Tasks (1 = never to 5 = full-time)

| | N | Mean | Std. Deviation |
|---|---|---|---|
| I am involved in handling issues related to projects or groups of projects | 239 | 3.47 | 1.068 |
| Before work on project deliverables begins I am involved in project plan reviews | 241 | 3.26 | 1.077 |
| I am involved in the improvement of my firm's or institution's internal processes | 242 | 3.26 | 1.071 |
| I am involved in resource planning | 239 | 3.19 | 1.139 |
| I am involved in the coordination of projects to achieve time, cost or resources efficiency | 241 | 3.11 | 1.142 |
| I am involved in reviews of projects or groups of projects | 240 | 3.05 | 1.179 |
| I am involved in business planning for the projects that the organization I manage is involved in | 241 | 2.98 | 1.167 |
| I coach or mentor project managers | 241 | 2.91 | 1.244 |
| I collect reports from projects | 240 | 2.89 | 1.214 |
| I am involved in identifying business opportunities | 241 | 2.75 | 1.196 |
| I am involved in the prioritization of projects | 241 | 2.75 | 1.200 |
| I am working in steering groups for projects or groups of projects | 241 | 2.63 | 1.282 |
| I am involved in resource procurement | 241 | 2.61 | 1.149 |
| I am involved in identification of bad projects in the organization | 242 | 2.46 | 1.181 |

Table 13    Differences between High and Low Performing Organizations

The reported "other activities" also differ between managers in high and low performing organizations. Managers in high performing organizations perform activities that are more:

- Strategic in nature
- Customer oriented, in order to develop value for clients
- Business related, as opposed to internal or administrative work.

Examples of reported "other activities" of managers in high performing organizations include:

> I am involved in working with the clients in setting the expectations for their projects after we understand what they actually need the project to do. What a client wants a project to do and the reality of what we can deliver given the clients' economic capability are many times two different things.

> I am involved in qualifications based selection—preparing qualifications packages, orchestrating qualifications presentations, scope development, contract negotiations for most projects in my programs and portfolio.

> Strategic Planning for IT is made yearly with Clients and my team of Coordinators.

> Provide the organisation [sic] an overview of opportunities and project portfolio and utilization.

> Taking programs through the stage gate process (manage core teams, prepare for stage gate reviews, etc.)

Managers in low performing organizations often report their "other activities" as being more administrative, such as documentation of standards and routines, or internal improvements.

Examples for managers' roles in low performing organizations include:

> Involved in defining and documenting standards, policies and guidelines for project and technology governance.

> Co-ordination of international projects and routines to make it easier to work with cross-border projects. Also development and training of personnel in the projects takes a moderate extent of my time.

Similarities between these groups were found in their roles for project selection and project prioritization.

### Middle Managers Roles in Program and Portfolio Management

The following describes the process underlying the roles listed in Table 3.

Prior to involvement in project-related activities, middle managers perform business planning and resource planning activities in relation to the organization's annual plan. Upon identification of new projects, they engage in project selection activities—which differ according to the nature of the organization—and accept, change, or reject a project. Companies subsequently start coordinating their activities as well as tasks to improve portfolio efficiency. They perform resource procurement and continuous project plan reviews for changes in resource requirements, in order to match resource availability (e.g., contingent on other projects) with the resource needs of the new project. This process continues throughout project execution, as every change in the resource requirements affects any one of the projects in the portfolio. Once the new project is in the execution stage, managers use regular reporting to identify troubled projects and to trigger remedial action or cancellation of a project. Throughout the execution stage, portfolio managers participate in internal steering group meetings, during which they disseminate portfolio-related reports. These reports are aggregations of project reports; portfolio managers then determine project priorities in collaboration with other members of the steering group. For those projects that are identified as being inefficiently managed, portfolio managers initiate reviews, coach project managers, or handle issues as otherwise required. To improve efficiency, they also engage in the organization's overall process improvement activities.

These activities are performed using a wide set of tools (e.g., aggregated red/yellow/green reports accumulated from individual project reports, organized into an overall list of risky projects and those with the most potential for impacting business results). Other tools used are time and cost information from enterprise resource planning (ERP) systems and profit and loss statements, as well as product roadmaps and strategic plans. The different roles are further described below.

## Portfolio Management-Related Roles Prior to Project Execution

### Business Planning

Middle managers within the companies interviewed engage in business planning as a result of previous strategic product or service decisions by upper management. Guided by their organization's strategy, the managers develop short- or medium-term business plans, which either reflect a company's existing strategy or serve as strategic responses to market pressures or competitor moves. These decisions lock out or lock in the organization in terms of future alternatives, for example, through development of a certain technology, entering of specific markets, or work with particular customers or systems (Ghemawat, 1991).

This is done at regular planning meetings, but also ad hoc in cases of larger marketing opportunities that require immediate response. For these business plans, managers develop the portfolio strategy, high-level product or service roadmaps, associated skills requirements, as well as implementation plans including schedules and budgets. This defines the operational activities needed to execute an organization's strategy, as summarized by one of the managers interviewed:

> A distinction which has just occurred to me is that (in my company) we use the term "portfolio" to define "the set of activities which are funded for the current year." We talk about "this year's portfolio," or "next years' portfolio"; whereas with projects and programmes [sic], we talk about them in life cycle terms—for example, as being in "defini-tion," or "delivery" and so on ...

Cooper et al. (2004b) point out the importance of product road-maps for New Product Development (NPD) portfolios. The roadmap outlines how management wants to achieve their desired objectives, both in terms of products as well as technology, and allows for identification of needed capabilities, which can then be planned for in terms of time and budgets. Clark and Fujimoto (1991), as well as Nobelius (2001), identify roadmap development as a critical balance of NPD project scope and its fit to the organization's project portfolio.

### Project Selection

Based on the business plans developed in the preceding step, manag-ers select a portfolio strategy and associated project selection criteria. A typical selection technique described by one of the interviewees was:

> We started with establishing the simple process to review new ideas and the flow of tasks that need to take place to validate them. We rapidly moved to the definition of the metrics by which projects could be fairly assessed against one another. We had five dimensions with level of investment required, attractiveness from an ROI/Payback standpoint, alignment of the project with the main company strategies, technical fit and chances of success. Each dimension had a series of criteria (1-7 max.) and all projects were then ranked in matrices to identify the most promising for next stages as well as the worse ones to stop rapidly.

Other interviewees emphasized the need for NPD products to complement existing projects in the portfolio, the fit of project objectives with organizational strategy, and the multi-dimensional aspects of economic decisions for project selection. Economic selection decisions were particularly impacted by the product's capability for growth, its capability to be sold across several markets, and the combination of time-to-market and expected returns.

A wide variety of project selection techniques exists. They can be categorized in numerical and non-numerical selection methods. Critical questions for project selection were raised by Nobelius (2001, p. 267):

- How well is the project related to the overall strategy?
- Can the project increase the knowledge and capability of the firm?
- When could this project be implemented?
- How dependent is the project on other subsystems?
- Is there any fallback or backup solutions if the projects fail?

Cooper et al. (2004b) identified the *strategic bucket* approach (described in the Literature Review chapter) as being associated with high performing NPD portfolios. Other authors, such as Meredith and Mantel (1999) favor weighted scoring models for three reasons:

- The possibility to include multiple objectives of all organizations involved
- Easy adaptation to changes in the management philosophy
- No bias towards the short run, inherent in profitability models.

An in-depth assessment of project selection techniques is beyond the scope of this report on roles and responsibilities. Interested readers are referred to Englund and Graham (1999), Dye and Pennypacker (1999), Blau, Pekny, Varma, and Bunch (2004), or Cooper et al. (2004a, 2004b, 2004c).

### Resource Planning

This role includes the development of a skills inventory needed to execute the project in the portfolio, as well as the processes for resource procurement decisions. It includes, among others, criteria for hiring new resources or using temporary external consultants, as well as internal or external training of existing human resources.

One of the managers who was interviewed described his resource planning activities related to portfolio management as follows:

> I have to decide who is going to work with what, balancing resources and secure new resources.

Another manager describes the problem of resource planning and synergy identification:

> On the inventory side, typically we find that there are too many projects going on and too few resources to focus on them, so most projects move at a snail's pace. In large organizations, it is not uncommon to find duplicate projects underway in different parts of the company.

Some of the organizations interviewed keep the level of permanently hired resources at about 80% of the needed resources for their portfolio work, and engage external consultants on a temporary project basis as needed. This ensures continuous utilization of their employed workforce, even in times of slightly lower than normal levels of business, and allows filling peaks of workload with temporary resources.

Engwall and Jerbrant (2003) identify the *resource allocation syndrome* as the number one issue in multi-project organizations, because of frequent re-assignments of resources to different projects in a portfolio. This is also described by the interviewed managers:

> Of course, you can move people between projects. However, if you do that too frequently, it becomes difficult to keep up with the schedules. It doesn't work. It causes delays, which lead to even more resources sent to the project. These resources then need to first learn about the project, so the quality starts to suffer.

> The limiting factor for the number of projects is the number of programmers I have for the moment.

Turner (2004) describes failure in planning of resource assignments as a problem caused by prioritization of projects and subsequent mechanistic allocation of resources to these projects. This leads to *all-or-nothing* effects, where high priority projects get all resources and lower priority projects none. He suggests a more balanced process to plan for resources in a portfolio context.

### Resource Procurement

This role ensures that the procurement of resources for the projects in the portfolio is done in an economical manner or otherwise aligned with the organization's strategy. As described in the paragraph above, some of the organizations interviewed have long-term relationships with specialists to engage them in projects on an as-needed basis. From a middle manager perspective, it lowers the risks for the portfolio because of well-known skill levels and economic conditions for procurement of individual resources. One of the managers in the interviews reported:

> We group projects and my role becomes one of ensuring that all-important projects have the resources from within our own set of competence. If we lack competence I have to procure it.

Survey respondents reported their responsibility for keeping and developing skills, knowledge, and capabilities of resources working within the program or the portfolio. One of the managers stated:

> I am responsible for setting annual business goals, target marketing, opening new program relationships, selecting alternative projects or clients, and keeping core expertise.

Little has been written in the portfolio management literature on this subject. Kendall and Rollins (2003) suggest identifying the *strategic resource*, which, more than other resources, contributes to the results of the projects in the portfolio and thereby causes a risk because of constraints in its availability. The value of resources with equivalent skills for the entire portfolio should be taken into consideration when making procurement decisions.

### Project and Program Plan Review

The role of middle managers in plan review is that of a critical assessor of the plans made by managers of projects and programs. This is a quality assurance activity to ensure validity, reliability, and credibility of an organization's plans. Organizations interviewed in this study use these reviews to assess the feasibility of the project or program in light of the organization's objectives and constraints. A statement representing the scope of this role is:

> I have to keep track of ongoing projects related to IT or projects that use resources within the IT department—to regularly follow up these projects regarding status, resource usage and delivery times

Questions asked during these reviews are, among others:
- Are the project and program objectives achievable with the current plan?
- Are the resources available, or can they be procured, for plan execution?
- Are resources used most economically?

In addition to reviews at the planning stage of projects, it is increasingly common to report project progress to management at project phase end. That is followed by stage gate (or toll gate) decisions by management on continuation or discontinuation of the project into the next phase. At these stage gate meetings, middle managers are involved for project and program plan reviews, as one of the interviewees reported:

> As a principle, we negotiate the budget on an annual basis, even if our perspective is one of three years. New opportunities or problems arise frequently in our business and must be handled appropriately. That can be through prioritizing within the portfolio, or by asking for more money. We use the steering group meetings for that, where a business case for re-prioritizing projects or increasing the number of resources is presented. Through that we keep middle management involved.

Cooper et al. (2000) describe the stage gate process in portfolio management.

## Program Management Related Roles Prior to Project Execution

### Identification of Business Opportunities

Middle managers involved in marketing activities are often also involved in the identification of business opportunities. Here, they take on a program management perspective to identify clients' business needs and develop solutions in the form of projects or programs of projects that fit both their organization's strategy and their client's needs. One of the interviewees reported on the changing role of managers in the identification of business opportunities:

> The program managers become more of engagement partners and they are expected to farm more business.

The business opportunities identified by the program manager are then subject to approval by the portfolio manager, or the Steering group, sales manager or owner of the firm in his/their role as portfolio manager. One respondent said:

> As the owner, I make the ultimate decision on which projects we will bid on and I review the planning and results of our associate project managers.

According to the organizations interviewed, this role often includes the breaking down of clients' business requirements into smaller entities, which are then translated into more technical requirements for a possible solution. These requirements are then taken to the manager's organization to assess their feasibility.

Frame (1994) describes the importance of understanding the customer's needs and requirements at this stage of a program. Mistakes at this stage are likely to become very expensive to correct at later stages in the program. He suggests involving analysts, who are not only versed in their technical and business arena, but also possess personality traits that help build credibility with a customer.

### Synergy Identification

Within this role, the manager identifies synergies across the program or portfolio, by identifying similar processes, tools or techniques, as well as existing solutions for some of the development tasks in the projects. Interviewees reported:

> We have a requirement to standardize among our products
> to the extent that 80% of them are common.

In what is basically a knowledge management issue, the manager is faced with identification and usage of existing know-how or solutions. A study by McKinsey (Ealy & Soderberg, 1990) revealed that over 40% of product design issues at Honda were already resolved in prior programs, which caused 30% of design time to be wasted solving problems that were previously solved. The role of managers is, therefore, not only to have insight in past and neighboring programs, but also to encourage project team members to actively seek synergies and ways to implement them. Synergies become a way to transfer knowledge between projects (Nobeoka & Cusumano, 1995).

### Resource Planning and Selection

This role includes planning for resources at the program level, which includes determining the resource assignment strategy across the projects in the program. It includes working with portfolio managers to determine the resource needs and capabilities, and supporting project managers in resource leveling, for them to develop reliable project plans.

A practical application was described by one of the interviewees:

> The programmers have one or two areas that they know best.
> They could not work on every part of the system. They work
> fastest if they are in their main area, so we try to have a mix
> of competences. We have three matrices, a resource matrix
> linked to a skills matrix (a spreadsheet that shows what they
> cover and what they do not cover). The third matrix is on the
> different systems areas and what skills are needed for those
> areas. Making a list saying this person knows about this area
> and another list saying what skills we have available for work.

The overall efficiency of the program is dependent on the allocation of human resources between projects in the program (Hendriks, Voeten, & Kroep, 1999). Payne (1995) describes the need for a balance of resource requirements from projects and resource availability in organizations, together with a practice of commitment of allocated resources to projects. The ability to select resources has been described as especially difficult for program managers in multi-project organizations, because of the numerous dependencies that exist, for example, between departments, subcontractors, project teams, and projects in the program (Danilovic & Sandkull, 2005). Because of that, Eskerod (1996) showed that program managers should do their "head-hunting" for the right resources in the pre-sales phase of a project.

Very large programs may suffer from a lack of resources in particular geographic areas. One manager reported in the interviews about their large infrastructure projects, which are large enough that they can subcontract all suppliers (and their machines) in a region and still have to look abroad to satisfy the demand from the program. A large proportion of his work is to solicit tenders and evaluate ways to attract new subcontractors from abroad.

## Program and Portfolio Management-Related Roles During Project Execution

### Identification of Bad Projects

Within this role, managers use a variety of information sources to identify troubled projects. These include project reports or consolidated portfolio reports (often using red/yellow/green indication for project status), cost and time performance measures against plan, and earned value results. These are complemented by reports on organizational results, profit and loss statements, cost, revenue, and utilization reports.

One of the managers interviewed described it as:

> The day goes by in monitoring projects, work with project teams, follow-up with the project managers on where we are in the project, especially the commercial aspects, such as money, final prices, etc.

A second manager described it like this:

> I am the manager of what we call a Value Management Office. This Office is responsible for supporting senior management decisions on Information Technology initiatives through value and risk analysis of proposals. We also manage all project management processes as well as appropriate project deliv-

ery reviews. We provide reporting to Executives of all IT projects on progress, status and risks.

Managers' ability to detect troubled projects is linked with the organization's communication system. An open exchange of performance results of projects and the organization's support of this process allows for corrective action in case of plan deviations. An open communications culture, together with contemporary portfolio management software that processes qualitative and quantitative information, allows the building of an early warning system to detect projects that deviate from plan at the earliest point in time. Müller and Turner (2001) showed the importance of communication for project success. They identified communication management as the Knowledge Area with the strongest impact on results in IT projects.

### Participation in Steering Groups

In this role, managers accept the ultimate responsibility for project success by being a project sponsor or member of the project steering group. A steering group is made up of representatives of a project's buyer, supplier, and sometimes also the subcontractor's management. Through work in the steering group, managers review plans, accept deliverables, and ensure the linkage between the project and the organization's strategy. In steering group meetings, managers are kept informed of project progress, decide on changes to the project, and are able to take corrective actions if projects deviate from plan.

One of the interviewees described these meetings as follows:

> The steering group meets on a monthly basis. There we go through our projects and activities from a company-wide perspective. Participants are management, plus product management and project managers of the important projects—those that cost most money. We use a simple reporting—where are we in accordance with the schedule and where not, how do we do money-wise, and whether we have an issue with the marketing organization that should get the product.

Karimi, Bhattacherjee, Gupta, and Somers (2000) showed through empirical research in the IT industry that the use of steering groups is positively related to an organization's success with its projects. Steering group meetings were also identified as arenas for political fights for resources (Guimaraes & McKeen, 1989; Eskerod 1996). Managers in these meetings work hard to get the best ranking and resources for their projects, as well as the most attention from top managers in order to succeed with their interests. The importance of these meetings is beyond the tactical level of the individual projects dealt with by the steering group. It is a meeting of strategic importance for middle managers.

This is supplemented by many other meetings that consume much of the middle manager's day, such as meetings with staff, stakeholders, clients, etc. for solving issues, sharing information, or negotiating agreements. As one manager reflected on his work:

> About 50% of each day is composed of meetings and developing relationships with senior executives of the customer organization. Some of that is normal communication, building of trust, and a way of setting customer expectations.

### Prioritization of Projects

In this role, managers determine the relative priority of their projects. The difficulties in doing this are explained by one of the managers:

> To sell a product earlier than our competitors, we need to have it in time. If the project gets delayed we may have to cancel it. We have to think twice before we prioritize. It has been shown again and again that projects that took too much time will never lead to something. Those that were successful were the quick and short projects. Because of that, we try to do things in small pieces and try to accomplish something quickly. Big projects, on the contrary, take such a long time that no one will have the product in the end. Competition is faster and faster.

Priority is assessed in regular intervals, so that projects can be stopped when other, higher priority projects should be pursued. Assessment of project priority is often done at stage gate meetings or regularly scheduled portfolio meetings, where decisions are made to continue with the current project or invest the resources in a higher priority project. One of the interviewees stated that:

> The outcome of the weekly portfolio management meetings is a set of spreadsheets that show the projects listed in priority order under each portfolio. We are currently running three different portfolios. This ranking of projects is used in the allocation of resources and the arbitration of those projects as they compete for resources, such as developers, development environments, testers, testing environments, etc.

The meetings described above are important for getting agreement on the ranking of projects, as well as selection and allocation of resources.

Cooper et al. (2000) describe the mechanisms of stage gate processes. Various prioritization techniques are described by Dye and Pennypacker (1999).

## Coordination of Projects

This involves the balance of time and resources to allow all projects in a program to be finished within the planned time frame. A change in the schedule of one project in a program has a knock-on (or domino) effect on neighboring projects, with impact on these projects' deliverables or resources. One of the interviewees described this as follows:

> If I say that a project starts in September and finishes in two years time, then this is dependent on another ten projects keeping up with their milestones and toll gates. If one project starts to slip, then this impacts all others. Therefore, it is important to keep the schedules. If a project starts getting delayed, then immediate action is required to recover the time lost, because this cannot be done at the end of the project.

In this role, managers coordinate the requests from project managers for changes in resource schedules or timings of tasks.

Engwall and Jerbrant (2003) showed that project schedules are often changed due to weaknesses in their planning. Within programs, a change in the schedule of one project has an additional effect on the neighboring projects, which either depend on the first project's deliverables or resources. Fricke and Shenhar (2000) argue that a certain level of stability should be maintained, so that the organization's projects could be completed.

## Collection and Aggregation of Reports

Middle managers collect reports from project managers and aggregate them for higher management and other stakeholders. Managers interviewed were provided with detailed and summary information. However, they also often collected further information that was not readily available in existing summary reports or databases:

> Much of the information is automatically provided. We have an Information System—a global IT system. It is updated with information from ongoing projects, so that we rarely need to collect data not available through the system. Then we have several forums where we meet and information from various projects is presented.

Turner and Müller (2004) describe the role of communication between project managers and middle manager and its importance for project success. They identified the information needs of middle managers, and the required communication from project managers. In further studies, they showed the cultural differences in this communication (Müller & Turner, 2004) and the impact of contract types on the quality of communication between project manager and middle manager (Müller & Turner, 2005).

## Initiation of Reviews

As follow-on from the identification of bad projects (described above), middle managers often initiate project and program reviews to assess performance and develop corrective actions as needed. As stated by one of the interviewees:

> I am responsible for the resource utilization of a pool of project managers. I perform periodic reviews of projects and rate the effectiveness of the project managers. I participate in project reviews at varying phases and ensure adherence to our project delivery process. I assist management in the evaluation of business cases for the portfolio.

A positive side effect of these reviews is their knowledge transfer between projects. (Kess & Haapasalo, 2002). Newell (2004) argues that reviews should be related to process and procedures, so that other projects could gain knowledge and understanding from these experiences.

## Handling of Issues

Here managers engage in the identification of possible resources for problem solution. As shown above, managers in high performing organizations devote significantly more time to this role than those in low performing organizations, as an R&D manager reported in the interview:

> Depending on the number of urgent corrections requested by the business side or the technical side, this is something you have to do. You put them on fast track and play down others that you now work on.

Issue handling can also comprise the removal of organizational obstacles by the middle manager, as suggested by one interviewee as follows:

> ... they have problems with other groups (in the firm) and things are not running smooth. Then I have to remove obstacles so they could focus on development and progress.

Jugdev and Müller (2005), in their review of project success literature, identified middle managers' predisposition towards a project, that is, their interest in project progress, as a Key Performance Indicator (KPI) of the future. Müller (2003) showed the correlation between high performing projects and middle managers' engagement in projects. Low performing projects were associated with little interest in project progress and associated issues-handling on the side of middle managers.

## Coaching of Project Managers

Due to their seniority, middle managers often coach project managers in their work. This spans project management-related areas to the wider organizational areas, such as politics or inter-organizational relationships. A department manager reported this as follows:

> Acting as a coach for the project managers and catalyst for making things going.

Englund and Müller (2004) describe a process for project managers to navigate in the political "jungle" of organizations, and how to use a project management office to foster project management work throughout the enterprise.

## Improvement of Processes

All managers interviewed were involved in the improvement of their organizational processes; as such, it can be viewed as a standard role of middle managers. One manager described the scope of these improvements as:

> I have to implement improvements, better measurement procedures, and stricter quality assurances.

In terms of time devoted to program and portfolio management tasks, this role ranked second after the handling of issues associated with projects or programs. Internal process improvement projects and organizational change projects have been described as especially challenging due to organizations' inertia, that is, their resistance to change and the associated obstacles in project implementation (Blomquist & Packendorff, 1998, Blomquist & Sandström, 2004).

# Summary of Managerial Implications

Organizations should adapt their governance structure to the needs of their environment and project types. Middle managers should be included in resource procurement, steering groups, and identification of bad projects and project reviews.

Middle managers' roles in portfolio management are intertwined with traditional line management roles and, in many cases, are executed by the same person. Program management roles are not as interwoven with line management roles and, therefore, can more easily be separated out as a standalone role or position in an organization.

In order to increase the chances of an organization's success, project-based organizations should use a hybrid structure consisting of program and portfolio management, which emphasizes:

- Handling of project-related issues
- Review of projects
- Work in steering groups
- Procurement of resources
- Identification of bad projects.

Implementation of the roles described in this chapter will allow organizations to handle the requirements stemming from the nature of their projects, the complexity of their organizations, and the need for an external, customer-oriented focus.

## CHAPTER 5

# Theoretical Implications and Conclusions

This multi-method study investigated the determinants for program and portfolio management practices in organizations, and the associated roles and responsibilities of middle managers. It took a TCE perspective, and used a qualitative study with nine interviews and a Web-based survey with 242 responses to develop a framework of program and portfolio manager-related roles of middle managers, and how they are determined by an organization's situation, given its degree of environmental turbulence and project types. The framework is shown in Table 3.

The research questions can now be answered.

Research question Q1 asked:

> How do project type and organizational complexity determine the use of project portfolio and program management in organizations?

This was tested through research hypotheses H1 and H2, which showed that program and portfolio management practices are determined by the complexity of the environment.

Higher complexity, expressed as the number of factors taken into account during decision-making, leads to the use of specific program and portfolio management practices (i.e., processes and tools), such as:

- Selection of projects based on the organization's strategy
- Prioritization of projects, and communication of the priorities
- Portfolio management tools to collect and disseminate information about the status of all high priority projects

- Reporting to steering groups using similar templates and metrics
- Decision-making in the best interest of the organization.

Higher environmental complexity appeared to be associated with clear roles for:
- Identification of business opportunities and business planning
- Project reviews
- Handling of issues
- Coaching of project managers
- General process improvement.

Roles appeared to also be dependent on project type. Organizations running projects with a high degree of organizational change content show more roles for:
- Resource planning
- Steering groups
- Prioritization of projects
- Handling of issues.

Long-term projects appeared to be associated with:
- More business planning
- Project plan reviews
- Bad project identification.

Formal responsibilities, like those for plan achievement or human resources management, were not related to environment or project type.

Research question Q2 asked:

*What are middle managers' practices, roles and responsibilities in program and portfolio management in successful organizations?*

High performing organizations were found to apply project and portfolio management practices, as well as bad project identification, significantly more than low performing organizations.

Project managers' reporting relationships differ also with organizational performance. In low performing organizations, project managers report to middle managers with program and portfolio management tasks, whereas in high performing organizations, they report elsewhere.

A summary table showing research questions, hypotheses, and results can be found in Appendix C.

The final model for environmental and project type impact on program and portfolio management practices, roles, and responsibili-

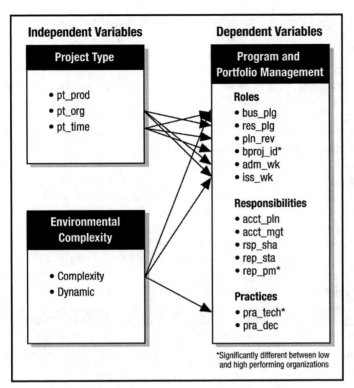

**Figure 10      Final Model**

ties is shown in Figure 10. It outlines the individual relationships between environmental complexity and project type variables with different program and portfolio management roles, responsibilities, and practice variables.

Modeling the relationship between roles and environmental variables showed that, across all organizations, requirements stemming from the environment (i.e., complexity and project type) are balanced through all six roles identified for middle managers. Low performing organizations, however, lack appropriate balance for the requirements stemming from complex environments, project durations, and product outcomes through adequate roles in the organization.

## Theoretical Implications

The results show a contingency between organizations' environment and their governance style. Especially complex environments, where "soft" projects are delivered to external customers, benefit from adopting portfolio management practices.

TCE's underlying assumption that different transaction types need different governance structures (Williamson, 1985) is supported by the research results. High performing organizations show more flexibility in adapting their governance to the requirements of their environment. They counteract the problem of bounded rationality in decision-making through specific processes and tools, as well as through focus on issues handling and business planning.

Program and portfolio management are seen as distinctive approaches to management, which primarily coexist in organizations due to the effect of these approaches on balancing different perspectives toward managing project-based organizations. A project can be simultaneously managed as part of program or portfolio (Archibald, 2003). So, its management is not exclusively a domain of the project manager. Aspects of goal or economic optimization from a wider organizational viewpoint are likely to influence the planning and execution of projects. That identifies the different perspectives of project, program, and portfolio managers towards project-oriented work in organizations (Turner & Müller, 2003); see

| Manager role | Perspective of the project as . . . |
|---|---|
| Project manager | . . . an agency for change and uncertainty management. |
| Program manager | . . . a temporary organization and a production function. |
| Portfolio manager | . . . an agency for resource utilization. |

**Table 14    Perspectives of Project, Program, and Portfolio Managers**

Table 14. Project managers use their project to bring about change in an organization or develop a new product. A project approach is used to manage the inherent uncertainty. Program managers, on the other hand, perceive projects as temporary organizations and as a means to produce the outcome of their program for the accomplishment of higher-level goals. Finally, portfolio managers perceive projects as an agency to utilize an organization's resource in an efficient way.

Looking at the combined roles of project managers, program managers, and portfolio managers described in the literature, as well as the interview results, it shows that:

- Project managers focus on the quality aspects of each stage, such as the quality in planning, development of products, and capture of knowledge.
- Program managers are more concerned with the individual project's fit in the overall program along the timeline, and the

overall fit with the permanent organization's strategic objectives.

- Portfolio managers are mostly concerned with the economic assignment of resources across various projects.

This reflects the well-known objectives of quality, time, and costs (focused on by project manager, program manager, and portfolio manager, respectively) at the level of the permanent organization, thus indicating the projectization of organizational structures. The alignment of roles within the organization can, therefore, be described as the project manager serving as the representative of the project, and the portfolio manager as the representative of the permanent organization, with the program manager bridging the two organizations through the sum of projects going on in a program in order to achieve the organization's objectives. This is summarized in Table 15.

| Phase | Project Manager | Program Manager | Portfolio Manager |
|---|---|---|---|
| Initiation and planning | Quality and feasibility of concepts and planning. | Timeliness of projects; fit to strategic goals. | Resource availability, capability, and costs. |
| Implementation and control | Implementing according to plan. Handover. | Integrating projects in overall time plan. Linking project outputs and inputs. | Optimizing resource allocation. |
| Closeout | Administrative closeout. Capturing knowledge and lessons learned. | Sharing knowledge and learning between projects. | Sharing knowledge and learning between resources. |
| Organizational perspective | Temporary organization (project) perspective. | Integrated temporary and permanent organization perspective. | Permanent organization perspective. |

Table 15    Organizational Perspective for Project, Program, and Portfolio Management

The findings resemble the "broker and steward" model, which was empirically developed by Turner and Keegan (2001). Their investigation into governance mechanisms in project-oriented firms identified two distinct roles, independent of the mix of large and small customers or projects in a firm. The first role is described as an extroverted, entrepreneurial broker, who builds and maintains the relationship of a supplier organization with a client. The program management role in the present study resembles much of the broker's role. The steward's role is to put together the network of resources to deliver the project. Similar to the description of the portfolio management role, stewards ensure the availability of the right person at the right place and time, taking into account the long-term objectives of the supplier and the interaction with neighboring projects and their resource needs. The project manager then manages

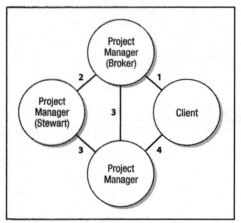

Figure 11    Broker-Stewart Model for Program and Portfolio Manager (after Turner & Keegan, 2001)

the process to deliver the project. Figure 11 shows this as a four-step engagement process for program and portfolio managers in external projects:

- Step 1: Program manager (as part of a sales team) identifies the business opportunity
- Step 2: Program manager engages the portfolio manager to decide on acceptance of the project and possible resource availability
- Step 3: Portfolio manager appoints the project manager, supported by information from the program manager
- Step 4: Project manager delivers the project to the client.

But why are there two distinct roles for broker and steward? In an attempt to answer this question, Turner and Keegan (2001) argue that the broker has to adapt to the external culture of the customer, whereas the steward adapts to the internal culture of the resource pool. That is equally important for the program and portfolio manager role, and adds to the justification for having these as two distinct roles.

The study showed that middle managers perform a variety of program and portfolio management-related tasks. In smaller organizations, in particular, these managers often have additional responsibilities that include department or product management. Several of the interviewees held staff positions without direct reports. These cases highlight the integrative task of middle managers, namely, the linking of different organizational entities into a cohesive whole. The nature of a program or portfolio as a cross-organizational grouping of projects puts these managers at the interface of otherwise separated organizational entities, such as those responsible for products, indus-

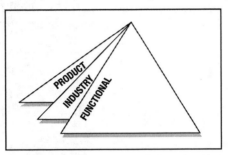

Figure 12    Perspectives toward an Organization

tries, or geographies (see Figure 12). Through this, the manager's role becomes one of organizational integrator: a coordinator of resources, consultant to management teams in various organizations, and potential escalator of issues across organizational boundaries.

Middle managers are pivotal in establishing these cross-organizational links by enabling the potential for generating and linking synergies in wide and diversified organizations.

## Suggestions for Further Research

The strength of the present study is in its multi-method approach, whose results matched those of existing studies and provided further insights into appropriate governance styles in different situations. The results, however, are on a global basis, and should be further assessed on a geographical and industrial level to develop clearer recommendations for organizations on how to best organize for the benefit of their results. Portfolio management's intertwined relationship with traditional line management roles, as seen through this study, opens the question of whether portfolio management could, in fact, be studied in isolation or only in combination with other line management tasks. Setting portfolio management tasks in relation to other managerial tasks would allow one to better understand these managers' rationale for decision–making, and provide one or more integrative pictures of the various tasks of middle managers.

## A Final Word

This report started with a statement about two recent trends:

- The increased use of projects as a way to do business in organizations
- The diminishing number of middle managers in organizations, which is contrary to the pivotal position they hold at the crossroads of strategic thinking and operational implementation.

The present study outlined the practices, roles, and responsibilities utilized by middle managers in successful organizations for coping with this situation. In outlining critical focus areas, the study highlighted middle managers' demonstrated flexibility in adapting their roles to their situation as a key factor for organizational success.

# References

Archer, N. P., & Ghasemzadeh, F. (1999). Project portfolio selection techniques: A review and a suggested integrated approach." In, L. D. Dye & J. S. Pennypacker (Eds.), *Project portfolio management* (pp. 207–238). West Chester, PA: Center for Business Practices.

Archibald, R. D. (2003). Managing project portfolios, programs and multiple projects. Proceedings of the 17th World Conference on Project Management, June 5–6, Moscow, Russia.

Association for Project Management. (2004). *Directing change: A guide to governance of project management.* High Wycombe, UK: Author.

Baker, N., & Freeland, J. (1975). Recent advances in R&D benefit measurement and project selection methods. *Management Science, 21*(10), 1164–1175.

Bettis, R. A., & Hall, W. K. (1981). Strategic portfolio management in the multibusiness firm. *California Management Review, 24*(1), 23–38.

Blau, G. E., Pekny, J. F., Varma, V. A., & Bunch, P. R. (2004). Managing a portfolio of interdependent new product candidates in the pharmaceutical industry. *Journal of Product Innovation Management, 21*(4), 227–245.

Blomquist, T., & Müller, R. (2004a). Program and portfolio managers: Analysis of roles and responsibilities. In D. P. Slevin, D. L. Cleland, & J. K. Pinto (Eds.), *Proceedings of the PMI Research Conference 2004, July 11–14, 2004 London.* Newtown Square, PA: Project Management Institute.

Blomquist, T., & Müller, R. (2004b). Roles and responsibilities of program and portfolio managers. In D. P. Slevin, D. L. Cleland, & J. K. Pinto (Eds.), *Innovations: Project management research 2004.* Newtown Square, PA: Project Management Institute.

Blomquist, T., & Müller, R. (2005a). *Practices, roles and responsibilities of middle managers in program and portfolio management.* Manuscript submitted for publication.

Blomquist, T., & Packendorff, J. (1998). Learning from renewal projects: Content, context and embeddedness. In: R. A. Lundin &

C. Midler (Eds.), *Projects as arenas for renewal and learning processes* (pp. 37–46). Norwell, MA: Kluwer Academic Publishers.

Blomquist, T., & Sandström, J. (2004). From issue to checkpoint and back: Managing green issues in R&D. *Business Strategy and the Environment, 13*(6), 363–373.

Brown, S. L., & Eisenhardt, K. M. (1995). Product development: Past research, present findings, and future directions. *Academy of Management Review, 20*(2), 343–378.

Burns, T., & Stalker, G. M. (1961). *The management of innovation,* New York: Oxford University Press.

Chien, C.-F. (2002). A portfolio-evaluation framework for selecting R&D projects. *R&D Management, 32*(4), 359–368.

Clark, K. B., & Fujimoto, T. (1991). *Product development performance: Strategy, organization and management in the world auto industry.* Boston: Harvard Business School.

Cohen, J. (1988). *Statistical power analysis for the behavioral sciences* (2nd ed.). Hillsdale, NJ: Lawrence Erlbaum Associates, Inc.

Cooper, R. G., Edgett, S. J., & Kleinschmidt, E. J. (1997). Portfolio management in new product development: Lessons from the leaders—II. *Research Technology Management, 40*(6), 43–52.

Cooper, R. G., Edgett, S. J., & Kleinschmidt, E. J. (1998). Best practices for managing R&D portfolios. *Research Technology Management, 41*(4), 20–33.

Cooper, R. G., Edgett, S. J., & Kleinschmidt, E. J. (2000). New problems, new solutions: Making portfolio management more effective. *Research Technology Management, 43*(2), 18–33.

Cooper, R. G., Edgett, S. J., & Kleinschmidt, E. J. (2002). Optimizing the stage-gate process: What best-practice companies do—II. *Research Technology Management, 45,* (6), 43–49.

Cooper, R. G., Edgett, S. J., & Kleinschmidt, E. J. (2004a). Benchmarking best NPD practices—I. *Research Technology Management,* 2004, *47,* (1), 31–43.

Cooper, R. G., Edgett, S. J., & Kleinschmidt, E. J. (2004b). Benchmarking best NPD practices—II. *Research Technology Management,* 2004, *47,* (3), 50–59.

Cooper, R. G., Edgett, S. J., & Kleinschmidt, E. J. (2004c). Benchmarking best NPD practices—III. *Research Technology Management,* 2004, *47,* (6), 43–55.

Crawford, L., Hobbs, B., & Turner, J. R. (2004). Project categorization systems and their use in organizations: An empirical study. In D. Slevin, J. Pinto, D. Cleland (Eds.), *Proceedings of the PMI Research Conference,* July 11–14, 2004, London.Danilovic, M., & Sandkull, B. (2005). The use of dependence structure matrix and domain mapping matrix in managing uncertainty in multiple project situations. *International Journal of Project Management, 23*(3), 193–203.

Duncan, R. B. (1972). Characteristics of organizational environments and perceived environmental uncertainty. *Administrative Science Quarterly, 17,* (3), 313–327.

Dye, L. D., & Pennypacker, J. S. (1999). *Project portfolio management.* West Chester, PA: Center for Business Practices.

Ealy, L., & Soderberg, L. G. (1990). How Honda cures "design amnesia." *The McKinsey Quarterly,* 1990, (1)., 3–14.

Elonen, S., & Artto, K. (2003). Problems in managing internal development projects in multi-project environments. *International Journal of Project Management, 21*(6), 395–402.

Englund, R. L., & Graham, R. J. (1999). From experience: Linking projects to strategy. *Journal of Product Innovation Management, 16*(1), 52–64.

Englund, R. L., & Müller, R. (2004). Leading change towards enterprise project management. *Projects & Profits,* ICFAI University Press, 2004, (November), 22–33.

Engwall, M., & Jerbrant, A. (2003). The resource allocation syndrome: The prime challenge of multi-project management? *International Journal of Project Management, 21*(6), 403–409.

Eskerod, P. (1996). Meaning and action in a multi-project environment. Understanding a multi-project environment by means of metaphors and basic assumptions. *International Journal of Project Management, 14*(2), 61–65.

Frame, J. D. (1994). *The new project management.* San Francisco: Jossey-Bass Inc.

Fricke, S. E., & Shenhar, A. J. (2000). Managing multiple engineering projects in a manufacturing support environment. *IEEE Transactions on Engineering Management, 47*(2), 258–268.

Galunic, D. C., & Eisenhardt, K. M. (1994). Renewing the strategy-structure-performance paradigm. *Research in Organizational Behavior, 16* 215–255.

Gareis, R. (2000). Program management and project portfolio management: New competences of project-oriented companies. *Proceedings of IRNOP IV, International Research Network for Organizing by Projects,* January 2000, Sydney, Australia.

Ghemawat, P. (1991). *Commitment: The dynamic of strategy.* New York: Free Press.

Glaser, B. G., & Strauss, A. L. (1967). *The discovery of grounded theory.* Hawthorne, NY: Aldine de Gruyter.

Gokhale, H., & Bhatia, M. L. (1997). A project planning and monitoring system for research projects. *International Journal of Project Management, 15*(3), 159–163.

Goold, M., & Luchs, K. S. (1996). *Managing the multibusiness company*. New York: Routledge.

Gray, R. C. (1997). Alternative approaches to programme management. *International Journal of Project Management, 15*(1), 5–9.

Guimaraes, T., & McKeen, J. D. (1989). The process of selecting information system projects. *Database, 20*(2), 18–24.

Hair, J. F., Anderson, R. E., Tatham, R. L., & Black, W. C. (1998). *Multivariate data analysis* (5th ed.). Upper Saddle River, NJ): Prentice Hall.

Hart, C. (1998). *Doing a literature review*. London: SAGE Publications Ltd.

Hendriks, M., Voeten, B., & Kroep, L. (1999). Human resource allocation in a multi-project R&D environment: Resource capacity allocation and project portfolio planning in practice. *International Journal of Project Management, 17*(3), 181–188.

Iyigün, M. G. (1993). A decision support system for R&D project selection and resource allocation under uncertainty. *Project Management Journal, 24*(4), 5–13.

Jick, T. D. (1979). Mixing qualitative and quantitative methods: Triangulation in action. *Administrative Science Quarterly, 24*, (4), 602–611.

Jugdev, K., & Müller, R. (2005). A retrospective look at our evolving understanding of project success. *Project Management Journal, 36*(4), 19–31.

Karimi, J., Bhattacherjee, A., Gupta, Y. P., & Somers, T. M. (2000). The effects of MIS steering committees on information technology management sophistication. *Journal of Management Information Systems, 17*(2), 207–230.

Kendall, G. I., & Rollins, S. C. (2003). *Advanced portfolio management and the PMO*. Boca Raton, FL: J. Ross Publishing, Inc.

Kerzner, H. (2001). *Project management: A systems approach to planning, scheduling, and controlling* (7th ed.). New York, NY: John Wiley & Sons.

Kess, P., & Haapasalo, H. (2002). Knowledge creation through a project review process in software production. *International Journal of Production Economics, 80*(1), 49–55.

Levene, R. J., & Braganza, A. (1996). Controlling the work scope in organisational transformation: A programme management approach. *International Journal of Project Management, 14*(6), 331–339.

Loch, C. H., & Bode-Greuel, K. (2001). Evaluating growth options as sources of value for pharmaceutical research projects. *R&D Management, 31*(2), 231–248.

Lycett, A., Rassau, A., & Danson, J. (2004). Programme management: A critical review. *International Journal of Project Management, 22,* (4), 289–299.

McGrath, J. E. (1982). Dilemmatics: The study of research choices and dilemmas. In J. E. McGrath, J. Martin, & R. A. Kulka (Eds.), *Judgement calls in research.* Beverly Hills, CA: SAGE Publications.

Meredith, J. R., & Mantel, S. J. (1999). Project selection. In L. D. Dye & J. S. Pennypacker (Eds.), *Project portfolio management* (pp. 135–168). West Chester, PA: Center for Business Practices.

Miles, M. B., & Huberman, A. M. (1994). *Qualitative data analysis* (2nd ed.). Thousand Oaks, CA: SAGE Publications.

Müller, R., & Turner, J. R. (2001). The impact of performance in project management knowledge areas on earned value results in information technology projects. *Project Management: International Project Management Journal.* Project Management Association Finland, *Norwegian Project Management Forum, 7*(1), 44–51.

Müller, R., & Blomquist, T. (2004). Analysis of roles and responsibilities of program and portfolio managers. In R. J. Harvey, J. G. Geraldi, & G. Adlbrecht (Eds.), *Proceedings of the Global Project and Manufacturing Management Symposium.* University of Siegen, Gemany, May 6–7, 2004.

Müller, R., & Turner, J. R. (2004), Cultural differences in project owner—manager communication. In D. P. Slevin, D. L. Cleland, & J. K. Pinto (Eds.), *Innovations: Project management research 2004,* Newtown Square, PA: Project Management Institute.

Müller, R., & Turner, J. R. (2005), The impact of principal-agent relationship and contract type on communication between project owner and manager. *International Journal of Project Management. 23,* (5), 398–403

Müller, R. (2003). *Communication of information technology project sponsors and managers in buyer-seller relationships.* DBA Thesis, Brunel University/Henley Management College, Henley-on-Thames, UK, www.dissertation.com.

Newell, S. (2004). Enhancing cross-project learning. *Engineering Management Journal, 16*(1), 12–20.

Nobelius, D. (2001). Empowering project scope decisions: Introducing R&D content graphs. *R&D Management, 31*(3), 265–274.

Nobeoka, K., & Cusumano, M. A. (1995). Multiproject strategy, design transfer, and project performance: A survey of automobile development projects in US and Japan. *IEEE Transactions on Engineering Management, 42*(4), 397–409.

OECD. (2004). *OECD principles of corporate governance.* Retrieved January 10, 2005, from www.oecd.org.

Partington, D., Pellegrinelli, S., & Young, M. (2005). Attributes and levels of programme management competence: An interpretive study. *International Journal of Project Management, 23*(2), 87–95.

Payne, J. H. (1995). Management of multiple simultaneous projects: A state-of-the-art review. *International Journal of Project Management, 13*(3), 163–168.

Pellegrinelli, S. (1997). Programme management: Organising project-based change. *International Journal of Project Management, 15*(3), 141–149.

Pellegrinelli, S. (2002). Shaping context: The role and challenge for programmes. *International Journal of Project Management, 20*, (3), 229–233.

Pellegrinelli, S., Partington, D., & Young, M. (2003). Understanding and assessing programme management competence. In *Proceedings of PMI's Global Congress 2003—Europe, May 2003, The Hague, The Netherlands.*

Pethis, R. F., & Saias, M. (1978). Metalevel product-portfolio analysis: An enrichment of strategic planning suggested by organization theory. *International Studies of Management and Organization, 8*(4), 35–66.

Platje, A., Seidel, H., & Wadman, S. (1994). Project and portfolio planning cycle. *International Journal of Project Management, 12*(2), 100–106.

Project Management Institute. (2003). *Organizational project management maturity model (OPM3®): Knowledge foundation.* Newtown Square, PA: Author.

Project Management Institute. (2004). *A guide to the project management body of knowledge (PMBOK® guide)* (3rd ed.). Newtown Square, PA: Author.

Remenyi, D., Williams, B., Money, A., & Swartz, E. (1998). *Doing research in business and management,* London, UK: SAGE Publications.

Schmidt, R. L., & Freeland, J. R. (1992). Recent progress in modeling R&D project-selection processes. *IEEE Transactions on Engineering Management, 39*(2), 189–201.

Scott, A. (1997). *Strategic planning.* London: Pitman Publishing.

Shenhar, A. (2001). Contingency management in temporary, dynamic organizations: The comparative analysis of projects.

*Journal of High Technology Management Research, 12, (2),* 239–271.

Simon, H. (1957). *Models of man.* New York: John Wiley & Sons.

Slevin, D. P., Cleland, D. L., & Pinto, J. K. (Eds.). (2004). *Innovations: Project management research 2004,* Newtown Square, PA: Project Management Institute.

Strauss, A., & Corbin, J. (1998). *Basics of qualitative research.* Thousand Oaks, CA: SAGE.

Thiry, M. (2004), For DAD: A programme management life-cycle process. *International Journal of Project Management, 22,* (3), 245–252.

Turner, J. R., & Speiser, A. (1992). Programme management and its information systems requirements. *International Journal of Project Management, 10*(4), 196–206.

Turner, J. R., & Cochrane, R. A. (1993). Goals-and-methods matrix: Coping with projects with ill defined goals and/or methods of achieving them. *International Journal of Project Management, 11*(2), 93–102.

Turner, J. R., & Keegan, A. (1999). The versatile project-based organization: Governance and operational control. *European Management Journal, 17*(3), 296–309.

Turner, J. R., & Keegan, A. (2001). Mechanisms of governance in the project-based organization: Roles of the broker and steward. *European Management Journal, 19*(3), 254–267.

Turner, J. R., & Müller, R. (2003). On the nature of the project as a temporary organization. *International Journal of Project Management, 21*(1), 1–7.

Turner, J. R., & Müller, R. (2004). Communication and co-operation on projects between the project owner as principal and the project manager as agent. *European Management Journal, 22*(3), 327–336.

Turner, J. R., (2004). *Managing web projects.* Aldershot, UK: Gower Publishing.

Wheelwright, S. C., & Clark, K. B. (1992). Creating project plans to focus product development. *Harvard Business Review, 70,* (2), 70–82.

Williamson, O. E. (1975). *Markets and hierarchies: Analysis and antitrust implications.* New York (NY): The Free Press.

Williamson, O. E. (1985). *The economic institutions of capitalism.* New York: The Free Press.

Yin, R. K. (1994). *Case study research: Design and methods* (2nd ed.). London: SAGE Publications Ltd.

# Appendix A

# Interview Instrument

1. Tell us about your company and the nature of its projects.
2. What is your role in the organization?
3. Do you use programs in your organization?
4. What are your roles in the management of programs?
5. What are your responsibilities in the management of programs?
6. Do you use project portfolios in your organization?
7. What are your roles in the management of portfolios?
8. What are your responsibilities in the management of portfolios?
9. What is your authority in the management of programs and portfolios?
10. What tools and techniques do you have to support your work?
11. How is your performance as manager being measured?
12. What is your relationship with neighboring organizations?
13. Describe one of your usual workdays.
14. Is there any other information that you see as relevant for our study?

# APPENDIX B

# Questionnaire Instrument

## Appendix B: Questionnaire Instrument

### Management of programs and portfolios

HANDELSHÖGSKOLAN VID UMEÅ UNIVERSITET

**U·S·B·E**

UMEÅ SCHOOL OF BUSINESS AND ECONOMICS

This questionnaire is part of a research project sponsored by the Project Management Institute (PMI®) on the roles and responsibilities in program and portfolio management.

Please answer the following questions in relation to your current daily work in the company, institution or other organization you belong to. Completing this questionnaire should not take longer than 20 minutes. For proper analysis of the data it is important that all questions are answered. Please submitt the questionnaire latest by December 10, 2004.

Information obtained from you will be held in strict confidence. No references will be made to specific individuals or names of organizations in future reports. The overall summary of the results will be shared with you if you so indicate at the end of the questionnaire.

There are 32 questions in this survey.

next >>

[Exit and Clear Survey]

# Management of programs and portfolios

This questionnaire is part of a research project sponsored by the Project Management Institute (PMI®) on the roles and responsibilities in program and portfolio management.

| 0% | 100% |
|---|---|

## A) Your role in the organization

**1: Please indicate to what extent of your time you perform the following tasks in your current position. (1= never, 2= to a small extent of my time, 3= to a moderate extent of my time, 4= to a large extent of my time, 5= full time)**

|  | 1 | 2 | 3 | 4 | 5 |
|---|---|---|---|---|---|
| The following three questions ask about your involvement in portfolio management. I manage a pool of resources - who's members are assigned to different projects - towards the effective achievement of my firm's or institution's strategy. | ○ | ○ | ○ | ○ | ○ |
| I manage a pool of resources who's members are possibly assigned to all projects in my firm or institution. | ○ | ○ | ○ | ○ | ○ |
| I manage a pool of resources who's members are assigned only to a defined set of projects in my firm or institution. | ○ | ○ | ○ | ○ | ○ |
| The following two questions ask about your involvement in program management. I manage a group of projects, which together achieve an outcome (product or service) that could not be reached with one project alone? | ○ | ○ | ○ | ○ | ○ |
| I simultaneously manage several projects which have no common objective. | ○ | ○ | ○ | ○ | ○ |
| I manage a single project. | ○ | ○ | ○ | ○ | ○ |
| Other (please specify below). | ○ | ○ | ○ | ○ | ○ |

❓ 1= never 2= to a small extent of my time 3= to a moderate extent of my time 4= to a large extent of my time 5= full time

## 1b: Please specify Other from above

```



```

<< prev    next >>

[Exit and Clear Survey]

86

# Management of programs and portfolios

This questionnaire is part of a research project sponsored by the Project Management Institute (PMI®) on the roles and responsibilities in program and portfolio management.

| 0% ■ | 100% |
|---|---|

## B) Your role in managing programs and portfolios

**1: Briefly describe your role in program and portfolio management within your firm or institution:**

**2: Please indicate to what extent of your time you perform the following tasks in your current position. (1= never, 2= to a small extent of my time, 3= to a moderate extent of my time, 4= to a large extent of my time, 5= full time**

| | 1 | 2 | 3 | 4 | 5 |
|---|---|---|---|---|---|
| I am involved in business planning for the projects that the organization I manage is involved in. | ○ | ○ | ○ | ○ | ○ |
| I am involved in identifying business opportunities | ○ | ○ | ○ | ○ | ○ |
| I am invlolved in resource planning | ○ | ○ | ○ | ○ | ○ |
| I am involved in resource procurement | ○ | ○ | ○ | ○ | ○ |
| Before work on project deliverables begins I am involved in project plan reviews | ○ | ○ | ○ | ○ | ○ |
| I am involved in identification of bad projects in the organization | ○ | ○ | ○ | ○ | ○ |
| I am working in Steering Groups for projects or groups of projects | ○ | ○ | ○ | ○ | ○ |
| I am involved in the prioritization of projects | ○ | ○ | ○ | ○ | ○ |
| I am involved in the coordination of projects to achieve time, cost or resources efficiency | ○ | ○ | ○ | ○ | ○ |
| I collect reports from projects | ○ | ○ | ○ | ○ | ○ |
| I am involved in reviews of projects or groups of projects | ○ | ○ | ○ | ○ | ○ |
| I am involved in handling issues related to projects, or groups of projects | ○ | ○ | ○ | ○ | ○ |
| I coach or mentor project managers | ○ | ○ | ○ | ○ | ○ |
| I am involved in the improvement of my firm's or institution's internal processes | ○ | ○ | ○ | ○ | ○ |
| Other activities related to your role in program and portfolio management (please specify below). | ○ | ○ | ○ | ○ | ○ |

? 1= never, 2= to a small extent of my time, 3= to a moderate extent of my time, 4= to a large extent of my time, 5= full time

**3: Please specify Other from above:**

<< prev    next >>

[Exit and Clear Survey]

## Management of programs and portfolios

This questionnaire is part of a research project sponsored by the Project Management Institute (PMI®) on the roles and responsibilities in program and portfolio management.

0% ▆▆▆    100%

**C) Your responsibilities in managing programs and portfolios**

**1: What is the title of your current position**

**2: Briefly describe your responsibilities in program and portfolio management in your organization:**

**3: Please indicate whether the following statements apply to your work:**

|  | Yes | No |
|---|---|---|
| I am accountable for the achievement of the annual plan of the organization I manage | ○ | ○ |
| I am accountable for the achievement of the plans of the programs or projects I manage | ○ | ○ |
| The responsibilities listed in the two questions above are shared between myself and other peer level managers | ○ | ○ |
| I have staff resources reporting to me | ○ | ○ |
| I have project managers reporting to me | ○ | ○ |

<< prev    next >>

[Exit and Clear Survey]

# Management of programs and portfolios

This questionnaire is part of a research project sponsored by the Project Management Institute (PMI®) on the roles and responsibilities in program and portfolio management.

0% ▬▬▬ 100%

## D) The organization

### 1: Please rate each of the following statements according to YOUR opinion, (1 = Totally disagree, 2 = Slightly disagree, 3 = Neither agree nor disagree, 4 = Slightly agree, 5 = Fully agree )

|  | 1 | 2 | 3 | 4 | 5 |
|---|---|---|---|---|---|
| The firm or institution I work for prioritizes their projects | ○ | ○ | ○ | ○ | ○ |
| The firm or institution I work for selects projects based on the organization's strategy | ○ | ○ | ○ | ○ | ○ |
| The firm or institution I work for communicates which projects are important | ○ | ○ | ○ | ○ | ○ |
| The firm or institution I work for uses a tool to collect and disseminate information about the status of all high priority projects | ○ | ○ | ○ | ○ | ○ |
| In the firm or institution I work for all reporting to Steering Groups is done using similar templates | ○ | ○ | ○ | ○ | ○ |
| In the firm or institution I work for similar metrics are reported for similar projects | ○ | ○ | ○ | ○ | ○ |
| Decisions about groups of projects are most often taken in face-to-face settings | ○ | ○ | ○ | ○ | ○ |
| Decisions about groups of projects are made as joint management decisions | ○ | ○ | ○ | ○ | ○ |
| Decisions about groups of projects are made in the best interest of the firm or institution I work for . | ○ | ○ | ○ | ○ | ○ |

**?** 1 = Totally disagree, 2 = Slightly disagree, 3 = Neither agree nor disagree, 4 = Slightly agree, 5 = Fully agree

### 2: Please tick Yes or No to indicate whether program or portfolio management is used in your orgnization

|  | Yes | No |
|---|---|---|
| The firm or institution I work for groups projects or programs together to facilitate the effective management of the work in order to meet strategic annual business objectives (i.e. uses portfolio management). | ○ | ○ |
| Related to question above: These portfolios of projects are managed by a single manager or group of managers | ○ | ○ |
| My organization groups related projects together to manage them in a coordinated way in order to obtain benefits and control not available from managing them individually (i.e. uses program management). | ○ | ○ |
| Related to question above: Is there a manager for such a program of projects? | ○ | ○ |
| The firm or institution I work for has a Project Management Office or Project Office (PMO / PO) , which is involved in program or portfolio management | ○ | ○ |
| Related to question above: I am part of the PMO or PO | ○ | ○ |

### 3: The project-based part of the firm or institution I work for achieves its annual plans in terms of ...

| | 1 | 2 | 3 | 4 | 5 |
|---|---|---|---|---|---|
| ... financial results | ○ | ○ | ○ | ○ | ○ |
| ... customer satisfaction | ○ | ○ | ○ | ○ | ○ |
| ... resource turnover | ○ | ○ | ○ | ○ | ○ |

❓ Ratings are: 1 = Totally disagree; 2 = Slightly disagree; 3 = Neither agree nor disagree; 4 = Slightly agree; 5 = Fully agree.

### 4: The project-based part of the firm or institution I work for achieves its program objectives in terms of ...

| | 1 | 2 | 3 | 4 | 5 |
|---|---|---|---|---|---|
| ... timely accomplishments of programs | ○ | ○ | ○ | ○ | ○ |
| ... stakeholder satisfaction | ○ | ○ | ○ | ○ | ○ |
| ... program purpose | ○ | ○ | ○ | ○ | ○ |

❓ 1 = Totally disagree; 2 = Slightly disagree; 3 = Neither agree nor disagree; 4 = Slightly agree; 5 = Fully agree.

### 5: The project-based part of the firm or institution I work for achieves its project objectives in terms of ...

| | 1 | 2 | 3 | 4 | 5 |
|---|---|---|---|---|---|
| ... time, cost and quality results | ○ | ○ | ○ | ○ | ○ |
| ... user requirements | ○ | ○ | ○ | ○ | ○ |
| ... project purpose | ○ | ○ | ○ | ○ | ○ |

❓ 1 = Totally disagree; 2 = Slightly disagree; 3 = Neither agree nor disagree; 4 = Slightly agree; 5 = Fully agree.

### 6: Over the last year, the following changes occured for the firm or institution I work for:

| | Increase | Same | Decrease |
|---|---|---|---|
| Revenue | ○ | ○ | ○ |
| Profit | ○ | ○ | ○ |
| Market share | ○ | ○ | ○ |
| Competition | ○ | ○ | ○ |

[ << prev ] [ next >> ]

[Exit and Clear Survey]

# Management of programs and portfolios

This questionnaire is part of a research project sponsored by the Project Management Institute (PMI®) on the roles and responsibilities in program and portfolio management.

0% ▮▮▮▮▮ 100%

## E) Demographics

The following data are collected for demographic purposes. All personal data will be separated from your answers prior to analysis of the questionnaire.

**1:**

Your age (in years): [                    ]

Number of years in business [                    ]

Number of years in current position [                    ]

Are you a certified project manager? [                    ]

Which country are you working in? [                    ]

What industry are you working in? [                    ]

In case you would like to receive a summary of the survey results, please fill in your email address: [                    ]

<< prev    next >>

[Exit and Clear Survey]

## Options: Internal or External projects (question F1)

**Internal projects (F1 = yes):**

### Management of programs and portfolios

This questionnaire is part of a research project sponsored by the Project Management Institute (PMI®) on the roles and responsibilities in program and portfolio management.

| 0% ▬▬▬▬ | 100% |

**F) The management of project groups**

Please pick an average project of your organization. One that you are familiar with.

**1: The project is internal to my organization, i.e. in the same company**

⊙ Yes

○ No

**?** This is a manadatory question. Please choose Yes or No.

**2b: The following questions ask about the Uniqueness of the project deliverables and the project risk. What is...**

... the project's budget (in US Dollars): _____

... the annual budget of your firm or institution (in US Dollars): _____

... the time from initiation of the project until work on the project deliverables begins (in months): _____

... the approximate percentage of cost of human work in the project (in percent): _____

... the total cost of accepted changes in the project (in US Dollars): _____

... the number of accepted change requests during the time of the project: _____

... your firm's or institution's budget in the year the project started (in US Dollars): _____

... your firm's or institution's budget in the year the project finished (in US Dollars): _____

... the number of tasks in the contract or Statement of Work: _____

... the length of the contract or Statement of Work (in lines): _____

There was a contract or Statement of work for this project. (Yes / No) _____

<< prev      next >>

[Exit and Clear Survey]

**External projects (F1 = No):**

## Management of programs and portfolios

This questionnaire is part of a research project sponsored by the Project Management Institute (PMI®) on the roles and responsibilities in program and portfolio management.

| 0% ▓▓▓▓▓ | 100% |

### F) The management of project groups

Please pick an average project of your organization. One that you are familiar with.

---

**1: The project is internal to my organization, i.e. in the same company**

○ Yes

◉ No

**?** This is a manadatory question. Please choose Yes or No.

---

**2a: The following questions ask about the Uniqueness of the project deliverables and the project risk. What is...**

... the project's sales value (in US Dollars):

... the annual revenue of your firm or institution (in US Dollars):

... the sales duration of the project (in month):

... the estimated costs of the project (in US Dollars):

... the approximate percentage of cost of human work in the project (in percent):

... the total cost of changes in the project (in US Dollars):

... the number of accepted change requests during the time of the project:

... your firm's or institution's sales in the year the project contract was awarded (in US Dollars):

... your firm's or institution's sales in the year the project was finished (in US Dollars):

... the number of tasks in the contract or Statement of Work:

... the length of the contract or Statement of Work (in lines):

There was a contract or Statement of work for this project. (Yes / No)

[ << prev ] [ next >> ]

[Exit and Clear Survey]

# Management of programs and portfolios

This questionnaire is part of a research project sponsored by the Project Management Institute (PMI®) on the roles and responsibilities in program and portfolio management.

| 0% ■■■■■■■ | 100% |

## G) Classification of projects

The following block of questions asks about the attributes of the projects in the organization you manage.

### 1: What are the attributes of the projects in the organization you manage?

|  | 1 | 2 | 3 | 4 | 5 |
|---|---|---|---|---|---|
| Project deliverables are tangible | ○ | ○ | ○ | ○ | ○ |
| Project deliverables are hardware | ○ | ○ | ○ | ○ | ○ |
| Project deliverables are software | ○ | ○ | ○ | ○ | ○ |
| Project deliverables are services | ○ | ○ | ○ | ○ | ○ |
| Projects aim to develop new products or services | ○ | ○ | ○ | ○ | ○ |
| Projects aim to develop our own or a client's organization | ○ | ○ | ○ | ○ | ○ |
| Projects aim to deliver a result to another firm or institution | ○ | ○ | ○ | ○ | ○ |
| Projects aim to update or maintain an existing system, product or service | ○ | ○ | ○ | ○ | ○ |
| Projects need mainly blue collar workers | ○ | ○ | ○ | ○ | ○ |
| Projects need mainly white collar workers | ○ | ○ | ○ | ○ | ○ |
| Project durations are often longer than a year | ○ | ○ | ○ | ○ | ○ |
| Project durations are often longer than three years | ○ | ○ | ○ | ○ | ○ |
| Project deliverables are unique for our firm (we have not done this before) | ○ | ○ | ○ | ○ | ○ |
| Every project is a combination of previous projects (we have done this many times before) | ○ | ○ | ○ | ○ | ○ |

**?** 1 = never to 5 = always

| << prev | next >> |

[Exit and Clear Survey]

---

94

# Management of programs and portfolios

This questionnaire is part of a research project sponsored by the Project Management Institute (PMI®) on the roles and responsibilities in program and portfolio management.

| 0% | 100% |
|---|---|

## H) The internal environment

The following block of questions asks about the way decisions are made within the organization you manage. For that a number of factors internal to your organziation are listed. You are asked to indicate the extent these factors are considered during decision making and how often these factors change. Here the question: Which factors are considered in the organization you manage when making decisions?

### 1: Organizational personnel component

| | Yes | Uncertain | No |
|---|---|---|---|
| Educational background | ○ | ○ | ○ |
| Previous managerial skills | ○ | ○ | ○ |
| Previous technological skills | ○ | ○ | ○ |
| Individual member's involvement and commitment to attaining system's goals | ○ | ○ | ○ |
| Interpersonal behavior styles | ○ | ○ | ○ |
| Availability of manpower for utilization within the system | ○ | ○ | ○ |

**?** Is this factor considered when making decisions in the organization you manage?

### 2: Organizational functional and staff units component

| | Yes | Uncertain | No |
|---|---|---|---|
| Technological characteristics of the firm's or institution's organizational units | ○ | ○ | ○ |
| Interdependence of the firm's or intsitution's organizational units in carrying out their objectives | ○ | ○ | ○ |
| Conflicts within organizational functional and staff units | ○ | ○ | ○ |
| Conflict between organizational functional and staff units | ○ | ○ | ○ |

**?** Is this factor considered when making decisions in the organization you manage?

### 3: Organizational level component

| | Yes | Uncertain | No |
|---|---|---|---|
| Objectives and goals of the organization you manage | ○ | ○ | ○ |
| Integrative process integrating individuals and groups into contributing maximally to attaining organizational goals | ○ | ○ | ○ |
| Nature of the product or serviceof the organization you manage | ○ | ○ | ○ |

**?** Is this factor considered when making decisions in the organization you manage?

## 4: How often does a factor change?

| | 1 | 2 | 3 | 4 | 5 |
|---|---|---|---|---|---|
| Organizational personnel component | O | O | O | O | O |
| Organizational functional and staff units component | O | O | O | O | O |
| Organizational level component | O | O | O | O | O |

**?** Rating: from 1 = never to 5 = very often.

## 5: New factors

| | 1 | 2 | 3 | 4 | 5 |
|---|---|---|---|---|---|
| How often do you consider new and different factors? | O | O | O | O | O |

**?** Rating: from 1 = never to 5 = very often.

[ << prev ]    [ next >> ]

[Exit and Clear Survey]

# Management of programs and portfolios

This questionnaire is part of a research project sponsored by the Project Management Institute (PMI®) on the roles and responsibilities in program and portfolio management.

0% ▬▬▬▬▬ 100%

## I) The external environment

The next block of questions asks again about factors for decision making. Now the factors external to your firm or institution are considered. You are asked to indicate the extent these factors are considered during decision making in the organization you manage. Here the question: Which factors are considered in the organization you manage when making decisions?

### 1: Customer component

| | Yes | Uncertain | No |
|---|---|---|---|
| Distributors of product or service | O | O | O |
| Actual users of product or service | O | O | O |

**?** Is this factor considered when making decisions in the organization you manage?

### 2: Suppliers component

| | Yes | Uncertain | No |
|---|---|---|---|
| New material suppliers | O | O | O |
| Equipment suppliers | O | O | O |
| Product parts suppliers | O | O | O |
| Labor supply | O | O | O |

**?** Is this factor considered when making decisions in the organization you manage?

## 3: Competitor component

| | Yes | Uncertain | No |
|---|---|---|---|
| Competitors for suppliers | ○ | ○ | ○ |
| Competitors for customers | ○ | ○ | ○ |

**?** Is this factor considered when making decisions in the organization you manage?

## 4: Socio-political component

| | Yes | Uncertain | No |
|---|---|---|---|
| Government regulatory control over the industry | ○ | ○ | ○ |
| Public political attitude towards industry and its particular product | ○ | ○ | ○ |
| Relationship with trade unions with jurisdiction in the organization | ○ | ○ | ○ |

**?** Is this factor considered when making decisions in the organization you manage?

## 5: Technological component

| | Yes | Uncertain | No |
|---|---|---|---|
| Meeting new technological requirements of own industry and related industries in production of product or service | ○ | ○ | ○ |
| Improving and developing new products by implementing new technological advances in the industry | ○ | ○ | ○ |

**?** Is this factor considered when making decisions in the organization you manage?

## 6: How often does a factor change?

| | 1 | 2 | 3 | 4 | 5 |
|---|---|---|---|---|---|
| Customer component | ○ | ○ | ○ | ○ | ○ |
| Suppliers component | ○ | ○ | ○ | ○ | ○ |
| Competitor component | ○ | ○ | ○ | ○ | ○ |
| Socio-political component | ○ | ○ | ○ | ○ | ○ |
| Technological component | ○ | ○ | ○ | ○ | ○ |

**?** Ratings: 1= never to 5= very often

## 7: New factors

| | 1 | 2 | 3 | 4 | 5 |
|---|---|---|---|---|---|
| How often do you consider new and different factors? | ○ | ○ | ○ | ○ | ○ |

**?** Ratings are: from 1 = never to 5 = very often.

**8: Do you have any comments on the roles and responsibilities in management of programs or portfolios? Please share some of your experiences.**

[ << prev ]  [ last ]

[Exit and Clear Survey]

## Management of programs and portfolios

This questionnaire is part of a research project sponsored by the Project Management Institute (PMI®) on the roles and responsibilities in program and portfolio management.

# Thank you.
## You have completed answering the questions in this survey.

Click on "submit" now to complete the process and add your answers to our records.

[ submit ]

If you want to check any of the answers you have made, and/or change them, you can do that now by clicking on the " << prev " button and browsing through your responses.

*A note on privacy*

The record kept of your survey responses does not contain any identifying information about you unless a specific question in the survey has asked for this. If you have responded to a survey that used an identifying token to allow you to access the survey, you can rest assured that the identifying token is not kept with your responses. It is managed in a seperate database, and will only be updated to indicate that you have (or haven't) completed this survey. There is no way of matching identification tokens with survey responses in this survey.

[Exit and Clear Survey]

# APPENDIX C

# Summary Tables

## Questionnaire Variable Descriptions

| | |
|---|---|
| X1–X7 | Role in organization |
| X10–X24 | Time spent on different tasks |
| X28–X32 | Accountabilities and responsibilities |
| X33–X41 | Management systems of programs and/or portfolios |
| X42–X47 | Use of program and portfolio management |
| X48–X50 | Portfolio's annual plan achievement |
| X51–X53 | Program's annual plan achievements |
| X54–X56 | Project's annual plan achievements |
| X57–X60 | Market changes |
| X61–X66 | Demographics |
| X68 | Internal/external projects |
| X69–X80 | External projects' TCE |
| X81–X91 | Internal projects' TCE |
| X92–X105 | Classification of projects |
| X106–X122 | Internal environment |
| X123–X141 | External environment |

## Computed variables

| | |
|---|---|
| X61c–X66c | Demographics |
| X143–X150 | Transaction Cost Economics (TCE) |
| X155 | Governance type of organization |
| X158 | Simple—complex dimension |
| X159 | Static—dynamic dimension |
| X160 | Role |

### Project type factors (from x92–x105)

pt_prod     Factor 1 = product orientation in project
pt_org     Factor 2 = organizational change orientation in project
pt_time     Factor 3 = project duration

### Role factors (from x10–x23)

ro_proj     Factor 1: Project coordination and issue handling
ro_bus     Factor 2: Business management
ro_res     Factor 3: Resource planning and procurement

### Management system factors (from x33–x41)

pra_tech     Factor 1: application of advanced technology and processes
pra_dec     Factor 2: decision-making (in groups)

### Succes variables (from x48–x56)

suc_portf     Portfolio success
suc_pgm     Program success
suc_proj     Project success
suc_all     Overall success

### Performance

LoHi_perf     Low and high performers: LoHi perf (0 = low, 1 = high)

## Performance Differences by Governance Structure

ANOVA analysis with post hoc Scheffe test showed a significantly higher performance in hybrid governance structure, that is, those using program and portfolio management.

**ANOVA**

Variable: suc_all

|  | Sum of Squares | df | Mean Square | F | Sig. |
|---|---|---|---|---|---|
| Between Groups | 19.957 | 3 | 6.652 | 15.052 | .000 |
| Within Groups | 102.536 | 232 | .442 | | |
| Total | 122.493 | 235 | | | |

Table 16     ANOVA of Differences in Success by Governance Type

Dependent Variable: suc_all
Scheffe

| | | Mean Difference (I–J) | Std. Error | Sig. | 95% Confidence Interval | |
|---|---|---|---|---|---|---|
| (I) ×155 | (J) ×155 | | | | Lower Bound | Upper Bound |
| .00 | 1.00 | −.33878 | .14472 | .143 | −.7463 | .0688 |
| | 2.00 | −.71522* | .11085 | .000 | −1.0274 | −.4030 |
| | 3.00 | −.29969 | .15822 | .312 | −.7453 | .1459 |
| 1.00 | .00 | .33878 | .14472 | .143 | −.0688 | .7463 |
| | 2.00 | −.37644* | .12609 | .033 | −.7315 | −.0213 |
| | 3.00 | .03909 | .16925 | .997 | −.4375 | .5157 |
| 2.00 | .00 | .71522* | .11085 | .000 | .4030 | 1.0274 |
| | 1.00 | .37644* | .12609 | .033 | .0213 | .7315 |
| | 3.00 | .29969 | .14139 | .037 | −.0174 | .8137 |
| 3.00 | .00 | .29969 | .15822 | .312 | −.1459 | .7453 |
| | 1.00 | −.03909 | .16925 | .997 | −.5157 | .4375 |
| | 2.00 | −.41554* | .14139 | .037 | −.8137 | .0174 |

*. The mean difference is significant at the .05 level.

Table 17    Scheffe Test on Differences in Success by Governance Type

## Performance Differences in Projects, Programs, and Portfolios by Governance Structure

The chart below shows the relative performance for:
- Projects (variable suc_proj)
- Programs (variable suc_pgm)
- Portfolios (variable suc_ptf)
- Overall organization (variable suc_all)

in the four different governance structures of:
- Neither program nor portfolio management
- Program management only
- Hybrid, using both program and portfolio management
- Portfolio management only

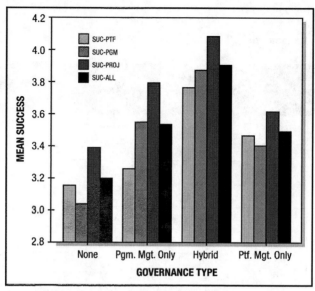

Figure 13    Project, Program, and Portfolio Performance in
             Different Governance Structures

## Summary of Research Questions, Hypotheses, and Results

| Research question | Hypotheses | Results |
|---|---|---|
| Q1: How do project type and organizational complexity determine the use of project portfolio and program management in organizations? | H1: Organization's perceived environmental complexity is directly related with the use of program and portfolio management practices. | Hypothesis confirmed. Organization's environmental complexity is directly related with the use program and portfolio management practices. |
| | H2: Different project types are correlated with different program and portfolio management roles and responsibilities. | Hypothesis partly confirmed. Different project types are correlated with different program and portfolio management roles, but not responsibilities. |
| Q2: What are middle managers practices, roles and responsibilities in program and portfolio management in successful organizations? | H3: Governance practices in program and portfolio management differ significantly between high and low performing organizations. | Hypothesis confirmed. High performing organizations scored significantly higher than low performing organizations in the application of program and portfolio management practices. |
| | H4: Middle managers' roles and responsibilities in program and portfolio management differ significantly between high and low performing organizations. | Partly confirmed. Middle managers in low performing organizations have project managers directly reporting to them. Project managers in high performing organization report elsewhere in the organization. |

Table 18    Summary of Research Questions, Hypotheses, and
            Results

# Appendix D

# Author Contact Information

Dr. Tomas Blomquist,
Department of Business Administration
Umeå School of Business and Economics
Umeå University
901 87 Umeå
Sweden

Tel: +46-(0)90-786-7722
Fax: +46-(0)90-786-6674
E-mail: tomas.blomquist@fek.umu.se

Dr. Ralf Müller
Department of Business Administration
Umeå School of Business and Economics
Umeå University
901 87 Umeå
Sweden

Tel: +46-(0)40-689-1312
Fax: +46-(0)40-689-1312
E-mail: ralf.mueller@fek.umu.se